2021 PMP Mock Practice Tests

PMP certification exam preparation based on 2021 latest updates - 380 questions including Agile

Yassine Tounsi

INTRODUCTION

Upgrade your self-study experience with an updated questions collection fully aligned with the new 2021 PMI updates.

This book equips PMP aspirants with an encompassing set of Mock tests to get fully prepared for the PMP certification exam.

The included set of tests is fully aligned with the latest updates of the exam to implicate best practices, the role of the project manager, and the growing importance of agile and other adaptive and iterative practices:

- **Domain 1 (People)**: 42 questions
- **Domain 2 (Process)**: 50 questions
- **Domain 3 (Business environment)**: 8 questions
- **Adaptive approaches/Agile**: 50 questions
- **Predictive approach**: 50 questions
- **Full Mock Exam**: 180 questions

Along with the real-world scenarios, the book presents detailed answers and explanations covering the most up-to-date solutions of critical topics and questions allowing you to gauge your readiness and avoid surprises on exam day.

The included tests were thoroughly created to guide you during your preparation and to reinforce you with everything you need to ensure exam-day success.

We provide further support and assistance through our private contact channels.

For any questions or inquiries please visit: ***www.yassinetounsi.com***

Domain 1 (People)

Question 1

Sam, a contracted project manager, is leading a project using a predictive approach. Ellie, the project sponsor, is disappointed with the progress so far, claiming that a critical deliverable has been overlooked. Although Ellie approved all project stages to date, she asked Sam to put the project on hold until she reassesses the situation. To reach an agreement, Sam decided to use arbitration and mediation as: (Select two)

    A. Dispute resolution techniques
    B. Coaching techniques
    C. Assisted negotiation techniques
    D. Direct negotiation techniques

Question 2

Shortly after joining a new organization as a project manager, you noticed a lack of collaboration within your team. What is the best course of action for creating a cooperative work environment?

    A. Conducting a soft skills development training
    B. Opting for a pull-based system for work assignments
    C. Organizing team-building activities
    D. Adopting an agile work approach

Question 3

Mark is a project manager who strives to build a work environment that promotes creativity, innovation, and ideas sharing. He sets up regular meetings with his team to discuss project risks and issues. What type of leadership is Mark applying?

    A. Transactional
    B. Interactional
    C. Transformational
    D. Laissez-faire

Question 4

Zad works as a project manager in a kitchen equipment manufacturer. Zad's superiors decided to adopt Lean practices, informing him to start preparing for this transition. What type of power is being used by Zad's superiors?

A. Legitimate
B. Referent
C. Expert
D. Situational

Question 5

Match the following techniques with the corresponding description in the table below:

- Brainstorming
- Benchmarking
- Focus group
- Nominal group

Technique	Description
A. -----------	Interactive group discussion facilitated by a moderator
B. -----------	Group discussion to quickly generate a large number of ideas
C. -----------	Group discussion to produce ideas and prioritize them through voting
D. -----------	Comparison of ideas, products, processes, practices, etc.

Question 6

Kim is in charge of a software development project that follows the Agile life cycle. During the execution of the project, Kim receives a request from the customer to alter a requirement. What should her response be?

A. Blocking the change request
B. Welcoming the change request

C. Avoiding the change request

D. Taking the change request to the change control board

Question 7

Fatima joins a project to replace a project manager who has abruptly left the organization. During the first week, she notices that her team members do not trust or support each other's ideas and that the work climate is counterproductive. According to Tuckman's model, at what development stage is Fatima's team?

A. Adjourning

B. Norming

C. Forming

D. Storming

Question 8

Richard is in charge of leading a ground-breaking medical research project. During a meeting with the project's sponsor on how to handle the project, Richard explains that he wants to encourage self-awareness, listening, and coaching. He adds that helping his project team grow is among his top priorities. What type of leadership does Richard intend to adopt?

A. Servant leadership

B. Authentic leadership

C. Transactional leadership

D. Transformational leadership

Question 9

Alicia is assigned as a project manager in a national bank. She decided to use the power/interest grid to plan stakeholders' engagement. How should Alicia deal with an interested stakeholder with little authority?

A. Monitor

B. Manage closely

C. Keep informed

D. Keep satisfied

Question 10
Daren is managing a branding project for a fast-food restaurant chain. During the project, two team members argue about a design task. Daren decides to conduct a meeting including both members and upon issue discussion, he finds that the best solution is to outsource this activity. Which conflict resolution technique did Daren use:

A. Forcing
B. Collaborating
C. Compromise
D. Smoothing

Question 11
Organizations often attempt to deliver projects with limited budgets and incomprehensive requirements. An Agile approach can be adopted to address such complexities. However, without proper communication, this approach won't achieve its goals. Under this context, how should a project manager communicate?

A. Informally
B. Formally
C. Frequently
D. Daily

Question 12
Angela works as a senior project manager for a medical devices firm, which has recently undergone significant organizational changes. Adam, one of her key team members, expresses his concerns to Angela about a new member, whom he believes lacks the technical proficiency to properly accomplish his assigned work. Since Angela has confidence in Adam's judgment, what should she do about this new team member?

A. Release the new team member

B. Nothing should be done since the team member has already been assigned

C. Provide the new member with training and mentoring

D. Keep the team member and reassign his tasks to someone else

Question 13

Shortly after starting a new project, you noticed that Gloria, who was a team member on your last project, is not as productive as she used to be. You invited her to a one-on-one meeting, where she admitted that her frustration is due to the fact that she had expected a performance bonus in the last project, but did not receive it. What theory is manifested in this situation?

A. Theory X

B. Theory Y

C. Anticipation Theory

D. Expectancy Theory

Question 14

After one month of project initiation, you notice that the sponsor is always late for your weekly meetings. However, you choose not to address their behavior. Instead, you document their tardiness in your meetings' notes. Which conflict resolution technique are you using?

A. Problem-solving

B. Smoothing

C. Information recording

D. Withdrawal

Question 15

You are in charge of an educational project. After analyzing the power of each of its four stakeholders, you find out that Monica and Markus have high power, while Ravi and Sergio have low power. For a deeper insight, you created the stakeholder engagement assessment matrix below. Based on your analysis, which stakeholder should be prioritized in terms of engagement?

Stakeholder	Unaware	Resistant	Neutral	Supportive	Leading
Monica			X		
Markus	X				
Ravi				X	
Sergio		X			

A. Monica
B. Markus
C. Ravi
D. Sergio

Question 16

Abigail is leading a project with remote team members in different geographical areas. During a virtual fortnightly retrospective meeting, she found out that some members either forgot, missed, or did not fully understand what was discussed in the previous meeting. What can Abigail do to address this issue? (Select two)

A. Ask all team members to try to speak English with a US accent
B. Create a new group norm requiring meeting attendees to raise their hands when they don't understand something
C. Record meeting sessions and send the recordings to everyone involved
D. Change the meeting schedule to weekly rather than fortnightly so that team members do not forget what has been discussed

Question 17

Nora is a PMP-certified project manager. She has a wide knowledge of project management and over 20 years of experience as a designer in the automotive industry. Her last assignment consisted in managing a group of designers to develop a new design for the upcoming car model. Knowing that her team trusts her decisions, which of the following powers does Nora possess?

A. Referent

B. Expert

C. Formal

D. Persuasive

Question 18

Since switching to the agile approach, Jackson has been encouraging his team to be self-organizing by allowing them to decide on how to execute their assigned work. What is the main aspect of a self-organizing team?

A. It gives more responsibility to the project manager

B. It gives more responsibility to the Agile team

C. It allows the team to deliver a working product without external dependencies

D. It gives team members higher visibility of the product

Question 19

Massimo works as a project manager for an organization that uses extrinsic motivators to improve team morale and productivity. What incentives should Massimo offer to his team in order to comply with his company's policy? (Select three)

A. Create an "Employee of the month" award

B. Offer a $10,000 bonus for the most performant team members

C. Allow team members to work on tasks they enjoy

D. Praise team members for their hard work

Question 20

The project Caitlyn is managing is nearly finished. When asked by a key stakeholder whether she was nervous about the project deliverables approval process, she said she was confident that the customer will be satisfied with the result. What can ensure the satisfaction of Caitlyn's customer?

A. The project's low running costs
B. How good Caitlyn's relationship is with the project's end-users and stakeholders
C. The efficiency of the warranty service
D. Conforming to project requirements and delivering value

Question 21

After 4 months of project work execution, Keagan noticed that the performance of some of her team members was deteriorating, while others continued to perform well. What should Keagan do to get the whole team back on track, given that this is jeopardizing the overall project progress?

A. Discuss the poor performance of certain team members openly with the rest of the team in order to come up with a joint solution.
B. Motivate underperforming team members by incorporating a competitive reward system that offers a bonus for top performers.
C. Avoid interfering in order to give team members a chance to improve their performance.
D. Identify the causes of bad performance, solicit systematic feedback and implement adequate solutions based on findings.

Question 22

Aicha presented a stadium construction project that she believes will benefit the community tremendously. Despite the mayor's agreement to carry out the project, Aicha encountered strong resistance from various stakeholders from the beginning. What is the best course of action to resolve this problem?

A. Aicha should create a Responsibility Assignment Matrix (RAM) to indicate which stakeholder is responsible for what aspects of the project and who needs to be consulted or informed.

B. Aicha should develop an organizational diagram that assigns each stakeholder to their appropriate project role, allowing or disallowing certain lines of communication.

C. Aicha should schedule a meeting with the concerned stakeholders to thoroughly explain the project, discuss and establish ground rules, ensure their involvement, and identify any personal or organizational issues that might surface later on.

D. Aicha should avoid contacting these stakeholders at the start of the project and instead create a "faits accomplis" to pressure them to support the project due to a lack of alternatives.

Question 23

As part of his job as a project manager, and through his multiple visits to many countries, Adolf learned that he needs to avoid being ethnocentric. What does ethnocentrism mean?

A. Being unfriendly to strangers

B. Inability to get adjusted to the culture of a new place

C. The belief that your own culture is superior to others

D. The initial shock of arriving in a foreign country

Question 24

Stephany is a new member of your latest project team. Thanks to her exceptional technical skills and ability to complete all her tasks in a timely manner, your company's CEO decided to promote Stephany to project manager. The CEO's behavior is an example of:

A. Herzberg Theory

B. Expectancy Theory

C. McGregor Theory of X and Y

D. Halo Effect

Question 25

As CEO, Li ensures that his employees have a healthy work environment with safe working conditions, job security, and rewarding salaries, with an emphasis on work appreciation. According to Herzberg, which of the mentioned above factors are examples of hygiene factors? (Select three)

A. Job security
B. Salary
C. Safe working conditions
D. Appreciation

Question 26

Jessica attended a meeting to finalize a procurement that was still in the negotiation stage. However, she noticed that discussions tend to drift to various irrelevant topics, with attendees occasionally going back to the meeting's main topic. What is this meeting missing? (Select two)

A. Minutes
B. An agenda
C. An objective
D. A facilitator

Question 27

Match the following communication methods with their corresponding advantages in the table below:

- Asynchronous
- Virtual
- Written
- Face-to-face.

Communication Methods	Advantages
A. ----------------------	Increases flexibility and reduces pressure
B. ----------------------	Builds connections and leads to more engagement
C. ----------------------	Decreases ambiguity and ensures commitment
D. ----------------------	Saves costs and limits interruptions

Question 28

Oliver is a project manager of a pharmaceuticals manufacturing project that follows a predictive life cycle. He makes sure to regularly communicate with stakeholders to collect their feedback and assess their engagement. At which stage do Oliver's stakeholders have the most influence over his project?

A. Initiating stages
B. Planning stages
C. Executing stages
D. Closing stages

Question 29

Daniel is the project manager of an e-commerce website development project. Upon the client's request, Daniel agreed to extend the scope while committing to the same delivery date. In order to achieve that, his project team must work 24/7. What's the best course of action for Danial?

A. Creating a night shift for his collocated team members
B. Hiring virtual teams that work in different time zones and schedules
C. Crashing the project
D. Using the resource leveling technique

Question 30

Huang is an agile coach who was invited to assist an organization in its transition to the Scrum framework. After examining the current situation, he finds out that the cross-functional team lacks a Single Point Of Contact (SPOC) to whom they can refer in case they have any questions about the product. Which of the following roles is missing in this situation?

A. Scrum Master
B. Sponsor
C. Product Owner
D. Project Manager

Question 31

You are managing a project using a hybrid approach. After one week of the first iteration, the customer informed you that they are dissatisfied with the deliverables. What should you do next?

A. Instruct the customer to submit a change request so that their dissatisfaction can be addressed
B. Use your soft skills to convince the customer that deliverables are conformed to project specifications
C. Investigate the cause of dissatisfaction and verify the deliverables
D. Implement adjustments and improvements in the next iteration

Question 32

The PMI Talent Triangle is a combination of expertise and skills that any aspiring project manager should develop to meet the evolving demands of their profession. The following elements make up the PMI Talent Triangle except:

A. Communication skills
B. Technical project management skills
C. Business management and strategic skills
D. Leadership skills

Question 33

Emma got assigned to manage a new project. Prior to the project kick-off, the project sponsor introduces her to the organization's C-level executives and reassures them that the project is bound to be a success. Who assumes responsibility for the project's success?

A. Project sponsor
B. C-level executives
C. Project manager
D. All of the above

Question 34

Sebastian is managing an agricultural project involving three stakeholders with high authority. By analyzing each of them, Sebastian identified Gerald as the one who has the most interest in the project. What strategy should Sebastian use for managing Gerald?

A. Manage closely
B. Keep satisfied
C. Keep informed
D. Monitor

Question 35

You are in charge of a construction project. When you first started acquiring resources, you asked Jack, a talent acquisition manager at your company, to conduct an MBTI (Myers–Briggs Type Indicator) Personality Test for the procurement manager position candidates. You requested that he only consider candidates who are comfortable approaching providers and communicating with them. Which personality type are you referring to?

A. INFP
B. INFJ
C. ISTJ
D. ESTP

Question 36

Communication is key to the success of any project. It is particularly important when it comes to building positive stakeholder relationships. Which is the best communication method to maintain and improve relationships with stakeholders?

  A. Interactive communication
  B. Written communication
  C. Pull communication
  D. Push communication

Question 37

Despite being an experienced project manager, this is the first time that Jakob is managing a remote team. He noticed that during meetings, he sometimes has to repeat what he's saying due to a bad Internet connection or a malfunctioning of his headphones. In a typical communication context, elements interfering with the transmission and understanding of Jakob's message are called:

  A. Medium
  B. Noise
  C. Decode
  D. Constraint

Question 38

You're in charge of New York's new bridge construction project. You were informed by one of the subject matter experts that during next July, all of the bridge construction work will need to stop taking into consideration past history of river flooding due to hurricane season. Thus, you agree with the expert and arrange to stop the work during that month. This decision is:

  A. Accept
  B. Transfer
  C. Mitigate
  D. Avoid

Question 39

Since leadership is crucial for project success, you join a training program to learn how to become a good leader. Which of the following activities should you learn to apply in order to become the leader you aspire to be?

A. Guiding, motivating, and directing your team
B. Improving your project's performance
C. Learning more about the specific domain of your project to be able to technically support your team
D. Learning more about project management through obtaining a PMP certification

Question 40

Advik manages a project with remote team members located all around the world. The project introduces cutting-edge technology that has never been used before. In this scenario, what is the key benefit of having a virtual team?

A. Widens the potential resource pool
B. Reduces the cost of setting up a workplace
C. Allows more inclusion of different cultures
D. The work continues around the clock

Question 41

Chris, who is a project manager, uses different power forms to gain support from project personnel. Which of the following are forms of power? (Select three)

A. Relational
B. Situational
C. Coercive
D. Seeking consensus

Question 42

Olivia learned through her professional experience that when interacting with her team, she should take into consideration the individual differences of each member. Individual differences in characteristic patterns of thinking, feeling, and behaving are referred to as:

A. Interpersonal skills
B. Personality
C. Seeking consensus
D. Integration

Domain 1 - Answers

Question 1 = A, C
Explanation: Arbitration and mediation imply reaching an agreement through the intervention of an arbitrator or a mediator. When direct negotiation fails to produce a satisfactory result, indirect or assisted negotiation methods like mediation or arbitration should be considered. An arbitrator examines the legal aspect of a dispute while a mediator attempts in good faith to narrow discrepancies. Litigation is another dispute resolution technique that involves going to court as a last resort when every other resolution method fails. Arbitration and mediation are not coaching techniques. The latter are used to help others be more effective and productive at work by setting an example, giving praise, providing constructive criticism, etc.

Question 2 = C
Explanation: Team-building activities foster a cooperative working environment when continuously implemented throughout the project lifecycle and especially in its early stages when barely any relationships among team members are developed. Carrying out soft-skills training could improve your team's ability to better communicate and collaborate, but it's less effective compared to team-building activities. Opting for a pull-based system for work assignments, i.e., a lean or a Kanban method, has the main purpose of improving productivity and decreasing delivery times rather than promoting collaboration. Also, following an agile approach should not be done just to increase collaboration among your team members, as your project may not be suitable for such an approach in the first place.

Question 3 = C

Explanation: Transformational leadership is when the project manager empowers their team by encouraging their ideas and creating an atmosphere of innovation and creativity. A transactional leader, however, is in favor of rules and procedures as they rely on their reward and punishment powers to run the team. Interactional leadership is a hybrid of transformational and transactional leadership. Laissez-faire leaders, on the other hand, adopt a hands-off approach by fully trusting and relying on their team to set their own rules and make decisions on their own.

Question 4 = A
Explanation: Legitimate power (aka formal, authoritative, or positional) is derived from someone's position or formal title. Zad's superiors' decision stems from their position as there are no indications that they used other forms of power in the described situation. Referent power implies a leader's ability to influence their followers through admiration, respect, or identification with the leader. Expert power, however, is based on employees' perception that their leader has a high level of knowledge or a specialized set of skills making them an expert. On the other hand, situational power implies being appreciated and respected for stepping up and saving the project or the team in a certain situation.

Question 5
A = Focus groups: involve an interactive group discussion facilitated by a moderator
B = Brainstorming: a group discussion to quickly generate a large number of ideas
C = Nominal group: a group discussion to produce ideas and prioritize them through voting
D = Benchmarking: involves a comparison of ideas, products, processes, practices, etc.

Question 6 = B

Explanation: Flexibility is one of the most important aspects of Agile: the scope of work can change in response to new requirements. An Agile, adaptive, or change-driven life cycle encourages collecting feedback from stakeholders on a regular basis. Unlike the predictive approach, and since changes should not be controlled, the Agile approach doesn't include or define a Change Control Board (CCB).

Question 7 = D

Explanation: Fatima's team is in the storming phase. Tuckman's team development ladder identifies five stages: forming, storming, norming, performing, and adjourning (PMBOK 6th edition, page 338). Storming is the most difficult and critical stage a team can pass through. Different individual personalities emerge during this phase, resulting in conflict and rivalry. At this point, the team performance will suffer tremendously as their energy is diverted to disputes and arguments. Forming is the first stage of a team's development where members are just beginning to know each other and form impressions. Team members usually avoid controversies or conflicts in this phase. The norming stage comes after storming; this is when team members begin to work together and trust each other. In the performing phase, teams begin to function as a unit; they get the job done smoothly and effectively without inappropriate conflict or the need for supervision. In the adjourning phase tasks are completed, the team breaks up, and members move on to other assignments.

Question 8 = A

Explanation: Richard intends to adopt a servant leadership style. The Agile Practice Guide distinguishes servant leadership with the following characteristics: promoting self-awareness; listening; serving teammates; assisting people in their development and growth; coaching rather than controlling; and promoting security, respect, and trust. Servant leaders prioritize the needs of others, helping them reach their best performance and potential. Authentic leaders focus on the self-development of themselves and their followers. Transactional leaders focus on supervision, organization, or performance, using incentives and penalties as motivation tools. Transformational leaders focus on motivation and creating an atmosphere of innovation and creativity.

Question 9 = C
Explanation: Alicia should keep stakeholders with high interest and low authority informed. As a project manager, she should proactively plan how to regularly communicate the project status to this stakeholders' group and check in with them to make sure they are not experiencing any issues or problems. Additionally, Alicia should closely manage stakeholders with high power and high interest, keep satisfied stakeholders with high power and low interest, and monitor stakeholders with low power and low interest.

Question 10 = B
Explanation: Since Daren chose to meet with his team members to discuss their conflict and make the best decision accordingly, then the situation implies problem-solving or collaborating, which leads to a win-win situation.
Other problem-solving techniques include:
- Forcing: which leads to a win-lose situation.
- Smoothing: which leads to a yield-lose situation.
- Withdrawing: which leads to a lose-leave situation.
- Compromising: which leads to a lose-lose situation.

Reference: Guan, D. (2007). Conflicts in the project environment. Paper presented at PMI Global Congress 2007.

Question 11 = C
Explanation: Agile frameworks are known for their frequent and straightforward communication where a project manager is continuously checking in with their team to accordingly decide what

could be alternatively done to improve the work pace and boost their team's morale. Daily communication should not be confused with daily standup. The daily standup is held by the agile team members who follow a scrum framework. The project manager or scrum master is not required to attend this meeting, but if they do, the daily standup meeting should not be their only channel of communication with their team. Whether you adopt a predictive or an adaptive life cycle for your project, you have to use formal and informal communication according to the situation.

Question 12 = C
Explanation: Angela should provide the new member with training and mentoring. When you realize a team member lacks the required competencies or skills, the first course of action is to use mentorship and training in order to improve their competencies. Doing nothing or reassigning their tasks to someone else will not help them improve their competency, which will only lead to their demotivation and negatively impact the project. Releasing the team member should be the last resort when every other option fails to put them on track.

Question 13 = D
Explanation: The Expectancy Theory states the following: employees believe that when they make more effort, their performance will be improved, leading to being rewarded, which they value, and this will motivate them to continue being productive. However, if they don't get rewarded, such in the case of Gloria, they lose their incentive to be productive. Theory X states that employees are incompetent, lazy, and untrustworthy. Theory Y, on the other hand, recognizes employees as being competent, responsible, and trustworthy. The situation describes neither Theory X nor Y since Gloria is described as being competent, but her performance declined as a result of not getting the bonus she was expecting. Anticipation theory is a made-up term.

Question 14 = D
Explanation: The unwillingness to deal with a conflict is referred to as withdrawing. This conflict resolution technique is acceptable when some time to cool off is needed in order to achieve a better understanding of the situation, or when the other party is unassailable or uncooperative. The situation does not imply problem-solving since the project manager didn't point out the issue to the sponsor in order to find a solution. The project manager didn't smooth the conflict either since there was no discussion to diminish their differences. Information recording, taking notes, or documenting the situation cannot be considered as a conflict resolution technique.

Question 15 = B
Explanation: The priority in engagement should be given to stakeholders with high power. Monica and Markus have high power, but Monica is Neutral, while Markus is unaware. Having a high powered unaware stakeholder is more dangerous than a neutral high powered stakeholder since they can cause a lot of trouble when they become aware at a late stage of the project. As the project manager, you should prioritize engaging Markus by sharing the project details with him. Then, you should try to win his support and bring him to the leading level if possible. Monica and Sergio should be your second priority. It's desired to have either supportive or leading high-power stakeholders. So, you need to make more effort to bring Monica to one of these two levels. On the other hand, even though Sergio's power is low, you need to work on moving him out from the resistant level since his power can change at any time throughout the project.

Question 16 = B, C
Explanation: To solve the issue, Abigail can create a group norm inciting attendees to raise their hands when they have questions.

She can also record meeting sessions and send recordings to all of the involved team members. Raising hands is practical in physical meetings as well as in video conferences. If a team member raises their hand to ask a question and still didn't understand a particular point, or if they missed part of the discussion, they can go through the recording. Abigail cannot force team members to speak with a US accent. If someone speaks with an unclear accent, then she could offer to provide them with training to improve their accent. The meeting schedule should not be changed just because people forgot the output. Meeting minutes and recordings are effective tools to address such an issue.

Question 17 = B

Explanation: Nora possesses expert power. Her PMP certification and years of experience in the automotive design field demonstrate that she has an advanced level of knowledge that prompts her team's respect. Other forms of power include referent, formal, and persuasive. Referent power is when team members respect or admire the leader for their personal qualities, such as their kindness or intelligence. Followers tend to admire these qualities, making them consider the leader as a role model. Formal power is derived from the position that one holds in the organization. Persuasive power implies a person's ability to provide arguments that influence people to take a particular decision or action.

Question 18 = B

Explanation: Unlike conventional teams, self-organizing teams do not wait for supervisors to assign them tasks. Instead, they determine which tasks must be accomplished, prioritize those tasks, and handle their schedules and deadlines on their own. Self-organizing teams tend to have a greater sense of ownership, engagement, and responsibility. A Cross-functional team, on the other hand, consists of team members with all the needed skills to produce a working product without external dependencies. Higher visibility of the product could only be developed by the product owner through backlog refinement.

Question 19 = A, B, D
Explanation: Extrinsic motivation is described as actions motivated by external factors such as grades, popularity, money, and praise. This form of motivation comes from outside of the person, as opposed to intrinsic motivation, which comes from inside of the person. Allowing each team member to work on things that they genuinely love to do presents a form of intrinsic motivation.

Question 20 = D
Explanation: It's not enough to complete a project on time and under budget. You need to deliver value by creating a suitable product for your stakeholders' needs. Customer satisfaction is about making sure that the people who are paying for the end product are happy with what they ultimately get. Conformance to requirements and usability of deliverables is the basis of customer satisfaction as they allow you to measure how well your product meets expectations.

Question 21 = D
Explanation: Keagan's objective should be to understand why a once competent team player is now struggling. The project manager should first recognize the symptoms, reach out to the underperforming team members, talk to them to try to find out the cause, offer whatever help they can, monitor and measure progress, and be sure to share feedback.

Question 22 = C
Explanation: Aicha should schedule a meeting with the concerned stakeholders to present the project, discuss and establish ground rules, ensure their involvement and identify initial personal and organizational issues is what Aicha should do. She can overcome

stakeholder resistance by simply listening to their concerns and suspending her own judgment of resisting stakeholders. The purpose is to see the project from the perspective of the stakeholders. The project manager should understand what drives and motivates the stakeholder.

Question 23 = C

Explanation: Ethnocentrism plays a significant role in the tension and division that exist among members of various ethnicities, races, and religious groups. It is the presumption that one's racial group is superior to another. Ethnocentric people feel they are superior to others merely because of their ethnic heritage. Clearly, this practice relates to problems of both racism and prejudice.

Question 24 = D

Explanation: The CEO's behavior is an illustration of the Halo effect. The Halo Effect implies making a decision based on a person's attribute or performance in one specific area. Stephany has great technical skills which gave the CEO the impression that she can be a great project manager. Apart from her technical skills, there is no tangible evidence proving that Stephany is able to lead a project. Herzberg's Theory recognizes two categories of workers' satisfaction factors: hygiene agents and motivating agents. Expectancy Theory states that people will behave based on what they expect as a result of their behavior. McGregor's theory states that management believes there are two types of workers: Y represents those who are self-motivated and enjoy their work and X represents those who dislike their work.

Question 25 = A, B, C

Explanation: According to Herzberg's Motivation Theory model (aka Two Factor Theory), there are two catalysts for creating job satisfaction: hygiene factors and motivating factors. Hygiene factors won't encourage employees to work harder but their absence will cause employees to become unmotivated. Hygiene factors include clean and safe work conditions, salary or paycheck, and job security. Appreciation is not a hygiene factor, it's considered a motivating factor.

Question 26 = B, D

Explanation: The meeting probably does not have a clear agenda nor a facilitator. An agenda organizes and structures a meeting's discussions, while a facilitator will ensure that an agenda is being followed and respected. Minutes of Meeting, aka MoM, are a summary of what happened during a meeting. They serve as a written record for future reference, thus they cannot be what caused this meeting to be chaotic. The meeting already has an objective; concluding a procurement in the negotiation phase. But, since no one is assigned to facilitate the meeting, it's probable that the objective was not appropriately communicated to all attendees in the first place, resulting in the described chaos.

Question 27

A = Asynchronous communication: Increases flexibility and reduces pressure

B = Face-to-face communication: Builds connections and leads to more engagement

C = Written communication: Decreases ambiguity and ensures commitment

D = Virtual communication: Saves costs and limits interruptions

Question 28 = A

Explanation: Stakeholders have the most influence and impact on a predictive project at its early stages. Stakeholder influence is mostly perceived in the early stages of the project. The project is flexible at this stage and can be changed and stakeholders generally take advantage of this. Once it starts to progress, the project takes on momentum and power of its own, thus, the cost of stopping it or altering its direction becomes very high. (Vogwell, D. (2003). Stakeholder management)

Question 29 = B
Explanation: Danial can rely on virtual teams that work in different time zones and different days of the week. Hiring resources from different geographical zones allows the project to operate 24/7 without overwork the team. Since Danial's project involves creating an e-commerce website, having virtual teams on the project is functional and practical. Construction or manufacturing projects, for instance, can't exploit the advantages of hiring a virtual team. However, they can opt for night shifts as a workable alternative. Crashing the project is used to add more resources in order to simultaneously work on different activities. Danial will certainly crash the project since he intends to accomplish more work within the same duration. But, crashing the project doesn't necessarily mean that the project will be running 24/7, which makes this choice not very precise. Finally, the resource leveling technique implies distributing workload based on resources' constraints. This technique is typically used in the schedule planning phase of a predictive project.

Question 30 = C
Explanation: The Product Owner, also known as the "voice of the customer," is the one in charge of ensuring that the cross-functional team creates value. The Product Owner ensures that the product specifications are communicated clearly to the team, through determining the Acceptance Criteria and ensuring that those criteria are met and satisfied. A Scrum team comprises three main roles: cross-functional team members, product owner, and team facilitator. The latter is also known as the project manager, scrum master, team lead, or team coach (Agile Practice Guide, page 41).

Question 31 = C

Explanation: The first thing you should do is listen to the customer, take note of the reasons behind their dissatisfaction, and verify the deliverables. Once this is done, you'll be equipped with all of the information you need to make the best decision. If you realize that it's just a misunderstanding or the customer is missing some details regarding the project deliverables, then you can simply use your soft skills to explain and convince them that the deliverables are good. However, if the deliverables do not meet specifications or require improvement, then you should schedule implementing changes in the upcoming iterations according to the priorities set by the customer. Since the project is hybrid, you may also need to ask the customer to submit a change request if out-of-scope work is requested.

Question 32 = A
Explanation: The PMI Talent Triangle is composed of three skill sets: business management and strategic skills, technical project management skills, and leadership skills. Business management and strategic skills are the knowledge and expertise that can help you set up your team in a way that produces better business outcomes. Technical project management skills include knowledge related to specific domains of the project. Leadership skills are the expertise involved in guiding, motivating, and directing others to reach a goal.

Question 33 = C
Explanation: While the project sponsor and eventually c-suite executives are accountable for the project, it is the project manager who assumes responsibility for achieving the project's objectives and overall success.

Question 34 = A
Explanation: According to the power/interest grid, stakeholders with high power and high interest should be managed closely.

Question 35 = D

Explanation: Since a procurement manager position requires an Extravert, ESTP would be a good fit. ESTP stands for Extraverted, Sensing, Thinking, Perceiving. ESTP indicates a person who enjoys spending time with others (Extraverted), who focuses on facts and details rather than ideas and concepts (Sensing), who uses logic and reasoning to make decisions (Thinking), and who prefers to be spontaneous and flexible rather than planned and organized (Perceiving). On personality trait measures, ESTPs score as Dominant, Flexible, Demanding, and Sociable. INFP stands for Introverted, iNtuitive, Feeling, Perceiving. INFPs prefer spending time alone, as they are often offbeat and unconventional. INFJ stands for Introverted, iNtuitive, Feeling, and Judging. INFJs are sensitive and reserved as they are of a private sort. They're also selective about sharing intimate thoughts and feelings and they prefer to be planned and organized rather than spontaneous and flexible. ISTJ· stands for Introverted, Sensing, Thinking, Judging. ISTJs are neat and orderly and are most comfortable in familiar surroundings. They often enjoy tasks that require them to use step-by-step reasoning to solve a problem.

Question 36 = A

Explanation: Interactive communication is the most effective communication method to maintain and improve relationships with stakeholders. Interactive communication is a real-time, dynamic, two-way flow of information. Push communication, on the other hand, is delivered by the sender to the receiver. It is recommended when the sender sends information that does not need an immediate response from the receiver. Emails are an example of this type of communication. Pull communication, such as blog posts, is delivered from the sender to a large audience. Here information is available for people to access when they need to.

Written communication is used to exchange formal or detailed information such as decisions, statistics, facts, etc.

Question 37 = B
Explanation: In a typical communication context, and within a sender-receiver model, the key components include Encoding of thoughts or ideas, a message as the output of encoding, a medium to transmit the message, and decoding of the message back into meaningful information. Noise is described as anything that obstructs the transmission and comprehension of a message.

Question 38 = D
Explanation: The decision of stopping work means that you are trying to avoid the risk rather than accept it. As the project manager, you made the safe decision to stop all construction work during hurricane season to avoid the risk of financial loss or putting your staff in danger. This risk response is suitable for threats with high priority, a high probability of occurrence, and a considerable negative impact. The decision can not be to mitigate because when you mitigate, you're attempting to reduce the threat's probability of occurrence and/or impact, and as the project manager, you have no control over river floods, plus you didn't take any action to mitigate its damage if it does occur.

Question 39 = A
Explanation: Leadership skills involve the ability to guide, motivate, and direct a team. This skill set may also include negotiation, assertiveness, communication, critical thinking, problem-solving, and interpersonal skills (PMBOK 6th edition, page 60). All other options can make you a better manager rather than a better leader.

Question 40 = A

Explanation: While employing virtual teams has many advantages, in this particular case, Advik takes advantage of the specialized skills a virtual team can offer. Without the use of virtual teams, the project would not have been feasible or cost-effective due to relocating team members or frequent travel. As a result, virtual teams expand the available resource pool.

Question 41 = A, B, C
Explanation: Seeking consensus is not a power of the project manager, it's rather an interpersonal skill used during conflict management or negotiation. The sixth edition of the PMBOK Guide recognizes the following fourteen powers of a project manager: Formal or Legitimate Power, Reward Power, Punishment Power, Expert Power, Relational Power, Informational Power, Persuasive Power, Ingratiating Power, Personal Power, Situational Power, Pressure-Based Power, Guilt-Based, Power, Avoiding Power, and Referent Power (PMBOK 6th edition, page 63).

Question 42 = B
Explanation: Personality can be defined as the unique way each individual thinks, feels, and behaves. Personality encompasses moods, attitudes, and viewpoints, and is most evident in social interactions. It involves both innate and acquired behavioral characteristics that distinguish one individual from another and can be observed in people's interactions with their environment and social groups.

Domain 2 (Process)

Question 1
Jack is managing a project with a distributed team, fixed budget, and tight deadlines. While adopting a predictive approach, what should Jack do to avoid any scope creep and keep his team focused on delivering a product that meets requirements?

A. Request the development team to skip all small requirements so that they can focus on big and important ones.

B. Hold frequent stand-up meetings with all of the development teams.

C. Ensure that all alterations to the scope are authorized through a formal process.

D. Prevent stakeholders from directly interacting with the development team.

Question 2
During the process of hiring an electrical engineer, Haley only conducted one behavioral interview. Later on, she discovered that the candidate's technical skills do not meet the job requirements. Therefore, Haley decided that henceforth she will support the recruitment procedure with a technical test and an additional technical interview. What risk response strategy did Haley apply?

A. Mitigate

B. Accept

C. Transfer

D. Avoid

Question 3
Azeez was asked to manage a flights' booking website. The airline requested that the website should be able to support one thousand visitors per hour. This condition is also known as: (Select two)

A. Requirement

B. Scope
C. Acceptance criterion
D. Deliverable

Question 4

Jacob is a senior project manager of an Enterprise Resource Planning project (ERP). In order to gather end-user feedback, Jacob discusses several ideas with his team and they draw the following diagram. What tool do they use?

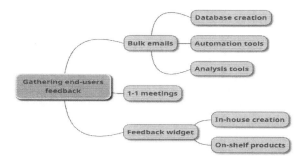

A. Mind map
B. Affinity diagram
C. Decision tree
D. Data representation

Question 5

After releasing the product, the organization faced poor quality claims from the customer. What kind of nonconformance costs the organization might encounter?
A. Internal costs
B. Appraisal costs
C. External costs
D. Risks and issue response costs

Question 6

Lara is managing a high-risk project, which has recently suffered from fluctuating performance and a high defect rate. During a meeting with the sponsor, they ask for an overview of work performance and where the project is currently standing. What report should Lara send to her sponsor? (Select two)

A. Quality report
B. Status report
C. Risk report
D. Progress report

Question 7

Astral Bank is well-known for offering excellent online services for its customers. As part of their new project, customers will be able to electronically submit a loan request. This project is in its third week of execution when the project manager discovers that an important resource has been over-allocated. This project is in need of:

A. Resource leveling
B. Resource smoothing
C. Resource calendar
D. Resource loading

Question 8

As an experienced project manager, John never initiates a project without conducting a kick-off meeting. What's the purpose of conducting such a meeting?

A. Informing and engaging stakeholders to ensure their commitment
B. Obtaining approval to proceed with project execution
C. Ensuring the allocation of the required project resources
D. Reassuring the stakeholders that execution is on track

Question 9

After one year of managing a fashion line project, and during the project completion and closure, Susan is faced with one key stakeholder's refusal to sign off on the deliverables due to non-compliance claims. Knowing that Susan adopted a predictive approach, what can she do to ensure stakeholder acceptance?

A. Issue a change request
B. Conduct a sprint retrospective
C. Change the SOW
D. Conduct a variance analysis

Question 10

Before the project starts, and after identifying all of the individuals and teams involved or affected by the project, Ella took a step further by classifying stakeholders according to their level of power, interest, and influence. This step is referred to as:

A. Stakeholder analysis
B. Stakeholder identification
C. Stakeholder management
D. Stakeholder engagement

Question 11

Lina is developing the business case of a green transportation project. To do so, she decides to use the SWOT technique. How should Lina apply this technique?

A. Follow a Plan-Do-Check-Act cycle (PDCA Cycle)
B. Assess the business model using expert judgment
C. Identify the project's strengths and weaknesses
D. Conduct a benefit/cost analysis

Question 12

Bella is managing an online e-learning platform. Her team is following the scrum method and every few weeks they release a new version including more features, user interface changes, bug fixes, security patches, etc. In order to avoid confusing users with the continuous changes, Bella decides to make the releases' information accessible to all platform members under the "news" section on the website. What type of communication is Bella using?

A. Push communication
B. Interactive communication
C. Pull communication
D. Proactive communication

Question 13

As the manager of a project with high uncertainty, Henry opts for the rolling wave method for the project planning. How is this method useful for Henry's project?

A. It will help him determine which activities are more important to prioritize them
B. It will help him organize the activities and tasks of his large project
C. It will help him determine the sequencing of a large number of activities
D. It will help him reach the proper level of detail in each work package at the right time

Question 14

Your project manager colleague canceled a Lessons learned review meeting due to time constraints. The potential consequences of this decision might implicate:

A. Issues faced through the project could reoccur due to the missed opportunity to identify preventive actions
B. Project management will get more difficult
C. Project cost will be greater
D. The project may not be accepted by the Project Management Office (PMO)

Question 15

Within a predictive approach, the _____ is the basis for cost estimation.
- **A.** Scope management plan
- **B.** WBS
- **C.** Resource management plan
- **D.** Cost baseline

Question 16
Foretheta is a Seattle-based IT company. Its latest project involves creating a mobile app for online training. Zoey, the project manager, decides to build a prototype for the mobile app. What added value do prototypes provide? (Select two)
- **A.** Allow for early feedback on the requirements
- **B.** Reduce project cost
- **C.** Complete the project faster
- **D.** Help to address ambiguities

Question 17
Raya is leading a project using a hybrid life-cycle approach. During a cost management planning meeting attended by the project sponsor and the CFO, Raya states that she will document that she is rounding to the nearest thousand and that she will be using weeks for resources' estimation. The above situation describes two elements of the cost management plan, which are:
- **A.** Units of measure & Control thresholds
- **B.** Level of accuracy & Rules of performance
- **C.** Units of measure & Control thresholds
- **D.** Level of accuracy & Units of measure

Question 18
Nora is managing a shopping center construction project. Following an inspection, the customer rejected some of the deliverables due to non-conformance to the acceptance criteria. What should Nora do next?

A. Assess the impact on project constraints

B. Document the reasons for nonacceptance

C. Issue a Change Request

D. Use her soft skills to convince inspectors to accept the deliverables

Question 19

Working in a predictive environment, you have decided to use a three-point estimation with a beta distribution to measure the cost of project activities. Which of the following formulas will you use?

A. (Optimistic + Pessimistic + Most likely) ÷ 3

B. (Optimistic + Pessimistic + (2 × Most likely)) ÷ 4

C. (Optimistic + Pessimistic + (3 × Most likely)) ÷ 5

D. (Optimistic + Pessimistic + (4 × Most likely)) ÷ 6

Question 20

David is a junior project manager working for a digital design agency specializing in branding and packaging. In his current project, he uses an approach that enables the team to share partially completed work with their clients to obtain early feedback, allowing them to modify the product accordingly. David is using a(n)_____ lifecycle.

A. Incremental

B. Predictive

C. Agile

D. Iterative

Question 21

Due to a financial crisis, your organization decided to pause all internal projects, including the project you are managing, to an undefined date. Knowing that you have a weekly meeting with a subcontractor who provides the majority of your project's physical resources, what is the best type of communication to inform them of the contract discontinuation decision?

A. Informal written
B. Formal written
C. Informal verbal
D. Formal verbal

Question 22
You are managing a biodegradable packaging project. Your team member informs you that they identified a risk implying that the printing machine may need maintenance before the end of the project. You estimate the risk's probability of occurrence as 10% and its cost as $5,000. This risk's expected monetary value is:
A. $500
B. -$500
C. $4,500
D. -$4,500

Question 23
Robert was informed by his project sponsor that he needs to complete the project one week sooner than the originally agreed-upon schedule. Knowing that Robert is using a predictive project management approach, what should he consider doing first to implement his sponsor's request?
A. Crash the schedule
B. Fast-track the schedule
C. Add duration buffers
D. Level out resources

Question 24
Mark is responsible for running the project quality assurance report. While reviewing a control chart, he observes nine data points in a row on one side of the mean. What should Mark do in this case?
A. Carry out a design of experiments

B. Make the necessary changes to the chart to reflect the new mean

C. Identify the assignable cause

D. This is the rule of seven, meaning it can be disregarded

Question 25

Harper, a senior project manager, joins an ongoing project following the resignation of its former project manager. To start guiding the team toward project success, Harper should:

A. Review the project budget to determine if more funding is required

B. Go through the project diary to consult the former project manager notes

C. Examine the project charter to be aware of the project goals and deliverables

D. Add a new activity to the project schedule concerning knowledge transfer

Question 26

Daniel is in charge of a mobile app development project. After facing some quality issues, Daniel and his team decide to use a tool to prioritize quality problems. Which of the following tools should Daniel and his team opt for?

A. Pareto chart

B. Ishikawa diagram

C. Control chart

D. Scatter diagram

Question 27

_____ can be predictive or adaptive. They provide the basic framework for managing the project.

A. Project management methodologies

B. Project life cycles

C. Project phases

D. Development life cycles

Question 28

Anas depends on time-boxing to help his team members avoid wasting time on shallow work and keep them focused on the main deliverables. What does time-boxing indicate here?
- **A.** A duration of intense activity within a specific release
- **B.** A time frame for executing specific activities
- **C.** Tight planning aiming to reduce the time required for an activity completion
- **D.** Setting a deadline for product delivery

Question 29

Gerard works for a company that develops mobile Apps. One of his latest projects involves the creation of an exercising app that syncs with another nutrition app to combine and analyze the data. As a result of a recent regulatory change, Gerard and his team are working on refining the backlog. The process of backlog refinement involves:
- **A.** The identification of the work items to be accomplished during the next sprint
- **B.** A board to keep track of the product and sprint backlogs
- **C.** A prioritized list of product requirements that is maintained by the team
- **D.** The gradual development of product specifications to meet the needs of the product owner

Question 30

You are in the phase of identifying and evaluating the risks of your construction project. One of the identified risks is so complex and ambiguous that you decide to transfer it to your program manager so they can make the appropriate decision. How did you respond to the risk?
- **A.** Transfer

B. Mitigate

C. Escalate

D. Avoid

Question 31

Sara is managing a project following a hybrid life cycle. Even though she made sure that all iterations have a balanced workload, she noticed that a particular team member was getting overwhelmed, while other team members seem to be doing fine. How should Sara address this issue?

- **A.** Inform upper management and request additional resources for the project
- **B.** Meet personally with the stressed team member to discuss ways to better manage their time
- **C.** Raise the issue with the team in the daily stand-up meetings
- **D.** Track the stressed team member tasks in a separate backlog for additional analysis and reporting

Question 32

Before taking a long leave, Amber informed Karla, who will be replacing her, that she should regularly calculate the project's Earned Value. Among the following options, what is the right description of an Earned Value?

- **A.** The difference between the budgeted cost of the performed work and its actual cost
- **B.** The value of the labor that has been employed on the project date
- **C.** The method of determining how much of the budget should have been spent based on the amount of work accomplished to date
- **D.** The amount of money that has been spent so far on the project

Question 33

Aaron is a graphic designer for a dairy brand. At the end of the iteration, he informs the project manager that he wasn't able to finish one of his assigned tasks due to an issue with his laptop. In order to prevent such a situation from occurring in the future, the project manager should:

    A. Discuss the issue during the demonstration session
    B. Address the issue during the following iteration planning meeting
    C. Handle the issue during the next daily standup meeting
    D. Discuss the issue during the retrospective meeting

Question 34

Grace is managing a high-tech project. During the planning phase, and to acquire physical resources, she received many proposals from qualified suppliers with whom she worked in previous projects, along with proposals from other suppliers. To compare between the different suppliers and make the best choice, which of the following tools or techniques should Grace use?

    A. Procurement performance review
    B. Selection criteria
    C. Procurement audit
    D. Make or buy analysis

Question 35

Upon receiving vendors' proposals for the new project you're managing, and in order to minimize the effect of your personal prejudice on source selection, you use a quantifying method for qualitative data. This method is referred to as:

    A. Weighting system
    B. Screening system
    C. Selecting system
    D. All of the above

Question 36

Velocity generally enables project managers to make accurate, but not totally precise, predictions concerning project planning. The term "Velocity" in scrum refers to?
  A. A team's sprint-by-sprint progress rate
  B. Project execution speed
  C. Team members' average capacity
  D. All of the above

Question 37
"Impediments" are usually evoked during the daily standup, and in some cases, they are thoroughly discussed during the sprint retrospective. "Impediments" refer to:
  A. Issues that block the Agile team's project completion
  B. Change requests
  C. External risks
  D. Problems caused by the product owner

Question 38
While monitoring the performance of a construction project under your management, you notice that it is likely to drift away from the planned schedule. You implement _____ in order to ensure that the project is fully aligned with the agreed-upon project baselines.
  A. Preventive actions
  B. Corrective actions
  C. Change request
  D. Defect repairs

Question 39
Managing an electric car manufacturing project, you're facing a complicated quality problem that you don't seem to understand its source and causes. You set a meeting with your time to discuss the matter and to initially trace the problem source back to its root cause. For that you use:

A. Pareto diagram
B. Chain diagram
C. Scatter diagram
D. Why Why diagram

Question 40
The following lists the story points of 8 tasks of an Agile project release: 3, 2, 5, 5, 8, 1, 3, 5. Given that your team velocity is 10, how many iterations are needed to complete all of the 8 tasks?
    A. 3
    B. 4
    C. 5
    D. 7

Question 41
Wilma was assigned as a project manager to organize a national chess tournament. The tournament has been planned and approved for execution. Three months separates Wilma from the big event, during which she will follow the scrum approach with 2-weeks long sprints. Before any work has been done, Wilma holds a meeting with the sponsor, project team, key contractors, and stakeholders. What kind of meeting did Wilma hold?
    A. Sprint planning meeting
    B. Kick-off meeting
    C. Status meeting
    D. Scoping meeting

Question 42
When Yasmine explained to her client the meaning of a story point in the agile methodology, she informed them that a story point can be defined as:
    A. The equivalence of WBS in the predictive approach
    B. An estimate of project duration
    C. An estimate of required efforts to complete a task

D. A score that is given to measure the clarity of the task

Question 43
Parkinson's Law is best described as:
   A. Work will fill all available time
   B. Starting work as late as possible
   C. More team members do not always produce more work
   D. Work will decrease as the team grows

Question 44
Which of the following is not a Cost-reimbursable contract?
   A. Cost plus fixed fee (CPFF)
   B. Fixed price incentive fee (FPIF)
   C. Cost plus incentive fee (CPIF)
   D. Cost plus award fee (CPAF)

Question 45
After 3 months of work execution, your sponsor faces a financial crisis due to COVID-19 so they ask you to immediately end the project. What should your next move be?
   A. Try to persuade the client to complete the project
   B. Talk to your management about the situation
   C. Start the close procurement process
   D. Start the close project process

Question 46
Ella is a Scrum Master. She used to attend or facilitate the different scrum events: sprint, sprint planning, daily standup, sprint review, and sprint retrospective. Which of the following options describes the sprint retrospective meeting?
   A. A meeting for refining product backlog items
   B. A meeting for discussing the negative and positive aspects of a sprint as well as any possible improvements

C. A meeting for defining and evaluating the work of the next sprint

D. A meeting held at the end of the project's last sprint

Question 47

Sacha is in charge of a children's hospital construction project. She received an email from her quality control team informing her that they're having numerous issues with one of the project vendors. As the project manager, what should Sacha do?

A. Penalize the vendor

B. Set up a meeting with the vendor and the control quality team

C. Terminate the contract and discuss with the control quality team the selection criteria of a new vendor

D. Raise the issue to the sponsor

Question 48

Mike was notified by his Management that they're sending a team of experts to conduct a risk audit. Even though Mike had already completed a risk review process without finding any shortcomings, the management insisted on proceeding with the risk audit. Which of the following statements are true about the risk audit and risk review? (Select two)

A. A risk audit is conducted to examine the risk response plan

B. A risk review is conducted to examine the risk response plan

C. A risk audit is conducted to investigate whether the risk response plan is being followed

D. A risk review is conducted to investigate whether the risk response plan is being followed

Question 49

One of your key team members leaves the project for personal reasons. You did not plan for such a scenario but you managed to get a replacement with the help of a staffing agency. However, you have to pay them a higher salary. This will result in extra costs which are going to be deducted from:

A. Contingency reserve
B. Project cost
C. Management reserve
D. Project budget

Question 50

Tessa is applying an adaptive life cycle for the project she is leading. How should she plan the project activities?

A. Plan all of the iterations work before the start of the project
B. Progressively elaborate the scope based on continuous feedback
C. Develop a high-level plan as the project progresses
D. Execute the project activities described in the statement of work

Domain 2 - Answers

Question 1 = C
Explanation: You can avoid Scope creep by adhering to the agreed-upon change management process. Change management processes have to be set upfront and should be very straightforward. Essentially, when a change is suggested, it should be reviewed, approved, or rejected and then incorporated into the project plan if it gets approved. Requirements shouldn't be skipped, small or big. Daily stand-ups and direct communication between stakeholders and your team cannot help you prevent scope creep from occurring.

Question 2 = A
Explanation: In the described scenario, the risk is hiring an unqualified engineer. Haley is aware of this risk so she took measures to mitigate it. Mitigation involves decreasing the probability of a risk occurrence (Haley's case), and/or lowering its impact it does occur. Even with the addition of a technical test and interview, there is still a chance that the candidate won't meet the job requirements (the test could be too easy or generic for instance), that's why "avoid" can't be the right answer.

Question 3 = A, C
Explanation: The condition of supporting one thousand visitors per hour is a requirement and an acceptance criterion for the project. A requirement is defined as "a condition or capability that is required to be present in a product, service, or result to satisfy a contract or other formally imposed specification." PMBOK Guide 6th edition (page 131). Acceptance criteria are conditions required to be met before deliverables are accepted. This condition can not be considered as a deliverable or a scope on its own. Deliverables refer to quantifiable products or services that must be delivered after a

project is completed, i.e., the flights' booking website. The project scope, on the other hand, is the overall amount of work required to achieve the project's main objectives.

Question 4 = A
Explanation: Jacob and his team used the mind mapping technique. In a mind map, several good choices are discussed and visually organized. The diagram is not a decision tree because it doesn't show or help in making the best decision among the different alternatives of gathering end-user feedback. On the other hand, the diagram is not an affinity diagram as it is not classifying a large number of ideas into groups. All of the mentioned tools are data representation methods, which makes "data representation" too generic to be considered the correct answer.

Question 5 = C
Explanation: Money spent during or after the project execution due to poor quality is referred to as the Cost of Non-Conformance. Internal and External Failure Costs are examples of Non-Conformance Costs. Internal failure costs are failure costs that are identified by the project team before the product gets released, such as Rework or Scrap costs. External Failure Costs, on the other hand, are failure costs identified by the customer, meaning costs incurred after the product is delivered to the customer, such as costs of Warranty work, Liabilities, Lost business, etc.

Question 6 = B, D
Explanation: Status and progress reports are examples of work performance reports (PMBOK 6th edition, page 112). Even though the project is at high risk and is encountering quality issues, the sponsor didn't explicitly request a detailed risk or quality report. The sponsor asked for work performance information to help them get more insights into the project and make better decisions. Status and progress reports could include information about the earned

value, trend lines and forecasts, reserve burndown charts, defect and risk summaries, etc.

Question 7 = A
Explanation: Resource leveling is the process of balancing resource use in order to address resource over-allocation. Resource smoothing, on the other hand, is performed to achieve a more consistent resource utilization over a period of time. In fact, resource leveling and resource smoothing are both resource optimization techniques, but they are used for different reasons. If the Astral Bank project should not exceed certain predefined resource limits, then smoothing will be the right technique. Resource calendar shows team members' availability. Resource loading is the total assigned hours of work divided by the number of hours required to complete it. In this case, the key resource is over-allocated, so their load is over 100%. The project manager could use resource calendar and resource loading as tools and techniques to help them achieve resource leveling.

Question 8 = A
Explanation: A project kickoff meeting is an opportunity to have the project team, sponsor, and stakeholders all on the same page. Its purpose is to communicate the objectives of the project, ensure the team's commitment to the project, and explain the roles and responsibilities of each stakeholder. The project kick-off meeting is usually associated with the end of the planning phase and the start of the project execution (PMBOK 6th edition, page 86). It's an informational rather than a decisional meeting, which means that the project manager doesn't seek approval to proceed with the execution during this meeting.

Question 9 = D
Explanation: The variance analysis is a technique used in the "Close Project or Phase" process to identify any deviation in

deliverables by comparing actual and planned behaviors. This method is used to determine the cause and magnitude of the difference between baseline and actual performance, as well as to retain control over the project.

Question 10 = A
Explanation: Stakeholder analysis refers to identifying and classifying all project stakeholders in order to manage them efficiently. Stakeholder management and engagement take place in the execution process group and they involve: communicating and collaborating with stakeholders to meet their expectations, addressing issues, and fostering appropriate stakeholder involvement (PMBOK 6, page 523). Since the question states that stakeholders were already identified and that the project didn't start yet, Stakeholder analysis is the right answer.

Question 11 = C
Explanation: SWOT stands for Strengths, Weaknesses, Opportunities, and Threats. It's a tool that project managers use to assess the opportunities and threats they might face, as well as their projects' strengths and weaknesses. Assessing the project's business model or conducting a benefit/cost analysis could be part of developing the business case, but they have a different purpose from the SWOT technique. PDCA is a quality management technique for controlling and continuously improving processes and products.

Question 12 = C
Explanation: The situation in question involves an example of pull communication. PMBOK defined three types of communication: interactive, push, and pull. Proactive communication is a made-up term. Pull communication is a communication type where access to the information is provided, however, the receiver must proactively seek out and retrieve this information. When the communication is

solely for informative purposes, pull communication should be used. It will have little to no impact on the project if the recipients do not read it. According to the PMBOK guide: "Pull communication is used for large complex information sets, or for large audiences, and requires the recipients to access the content at their own discretion subject to security procedures. These methods include web portals, intranet sites, e-learning, lessons learned databases, or knowledge repositories." The PMBOK Guide, 6th Edition, Page 374.

Question 13 = D
Explanation: Rolling wave planning is a project management method that includes a gradual elaboration of details to the Work Breakdown Structure (WBS) over time. Near-term deliverables are decomposed into individual components (work packages) that are broken down to the greatest degree of detail. Long-term deliverables, on the other hand, are identified more broadly. In this way, rolling wave planning allows work to progress on current and near-term deliverables while planning for potential work packages continues. The Rolling wave method is used to address uncertainty rather than prioritizing, organizing, or sequencing activities.

Question 14 = A
Explanation: The knowledge acquired from the process of carrying out a project is referred to as "lessons learned." This covers both the positive and negative aspects. The aim is to replicate good practices and avoid repeating errors. By failing to examine or go over past lessons learned, the project manager risks making the same errors as previous projects. The reason being, the earlier the lessons are identified and embedded into a project, the more value they will provide. So ideally, a project manager should conduct reviews on an ongoing basis to allow for continuous improvement. Such review will capture in-depth inputs from the project team, sponsors, stakeholders, etc. Capturing and going over lessons learned on a

regular basis helps keep the project on track. In the long term, it will also help organizations continuously develop and enhance the way they conduct projects.

Question 15 = B
Explanation: Since it includes all of the project deliverables as well as the control accounts associated with work package elements, the work breakdown structure (WBS) acts as the foundation of cost estimates.

Question 16 = A, D
Explanation: Prototyping is a technique used to collect early feedback on the requirements for further refinement and clarification, along with clarifying ambiguities. The development of the prototype can either increase the project cost and duration or reduce them thanks to the results it brings.

Question 17 = D
Explanation: Raya's statement describes the level of accuracy and units of measure: The rounding precision represents the level of accuracy, i.e., the nearest thousand, while the units of measure depict how to measure resources, i.e., weeks. In the described situation, Raya didn't set any threshold or rule for performance.

Question 18 = B
Explanation: First, Nora should document the reasons for nonacceptance. Then, she must meet with her team to assess the impact of the deliverables rejection on the project constraints, e.g., schedule and budget, and eventually issue a change request in order to align those nonconforming deliverables with the predefined acceptance criteria. It's not appropriate to try to influence the inspectors' decisions.

Question 19 = D

Explanation: The three-point estimation formula using a beta (weighted average) distribution is as follows: (Optimistic + Pessimistic + (4 × Most likely)) ÷ 6. In contrast, the three-point estimation formula that uses a triangular distribution (simple average) is as follows: (Optimistic + Pessimistic + Most likely) ÷ 3.

Question 20 = D
Explanation: Iterative life cycles focus on developing the product through a series of repeated cycles that successively improve or add functionality to the product by incorporating stakeholders' feedback. The iterative life cycle model differs from the incremental life cycle model in that change is expected. In fact, change is a necessary part of this model. (Source: Effective Project Management Traditional, Agile, Extreme, Hybrid by Robert K. Wysocki, page 49). An adaptive or agile life cycle is also change-driven as the iterative life cycle. Yet, it requires ongoing stakeholder/client engagement and the use of backlogs (including product requirements and user stories) to reflect their current needs.

Question 21 = B
Explanation: When dealing with complex issues, such as updating a plan or dealing with legal matters, it would be best to record discussions and decisions using a formal written format. According to the PMBOK Page 499 "The buyer, usually through its authorized procurement administrator, provides the seller with formal written notice that the contract has been completed. Requirements for formal procurement closure are usually defined in the terms and conditions of the contract".

Question 22 = B
Explanation: As a statistical technique, the Expected Monetary Value (EMV) is used to quantify risks and calculate the contingency reserve for risk management purposes. The formula for calculating the expected monetary value is multiplying the probability with the

impact of the concerned risk. Since the opportunities are expressed as positive values and threats or costs as negative values, incorporating the values gives the following result: $10\% \times -\$5,000 = -\$500$.

Question 23 = B
Explanation: In this case, one of two schedule compression techniques must be used: crashing or fast-tracking. Crashing the schedule involves compressing the schedule by adding more resources to the project. However, fast-tracking is the method of performing originally sequential activities in a simultaneous way instead. When possible, select the lowest-cost option first, which would be fast-tracking.

Question 24 = C
Explanation: The rule of seven states that if seven or more consecutive measurements are on one side of the mean, then there's an assignable cause that needs investigation.

Question 25 = C
Explanation: The project manager should be fully aware of the project's purpose, priorities, and deliverables in order to effectively lead the project. After examining the project goals and deliverables included in the project charter, Harper should create a transition plan to help the project team cope with the unexpected change, reassess what has been accomplished so far, and maintain commitment to the project goals and priorities.

Question 26 = A
Explanation: Pareto diagram consists of a vertical bar chart mainly used to highlight the most important sources of a problem out of the total number of effects, aiming to take appropriate measures to improve a certain issue or situation. Typically, it will be organized into categories that measure either frequencies or consequences.

Question 27 = B
Explanation: A project life cycle can be either predictive or adaptive. Within a project life cycle, there are generally one or several phases for developing a product, service, or result. These are called a development life cycle. Development life cycles can be predictive, iterative, incremental, adaptive, or hybrid (PMBOK 6th edition, page 19). Project phases can be sequential, iterative, or overlapping.

Question 28 = B
Explanation: Timeboxing is an important agile task management technique. It has been defined by the Agile Alliance as an agreed-upon period of time to achieve a goal. Under a traditional project that follows a predictive life cycle, time is considered as an adjustable variable for the ultimate purpose of achieving the predefined project scope.

Question 29 = D
Explanation: Backlog refinement refers to the progressive elaboration of project requirements where the Agile team collaboratively integrates reviews and updates with the sole purpose of meeting and satisfying the customer and product owner's needs. The identification of the work items to be accomplished during the next sprint is carried out during the sprint planning. The backlog is a prioritized list of product requirements that is maintained by the team. An information radiator or a Kanban board helps to keep track of the product and sprint backlogs.

Question 30 = C
Explanation: In the described scenario, you have escalated the risk to your program manager. When a threat is considered to be outside of the project scope or when the appropriate response exceeds the project manager's authority, risk escalation is the suitable risk

response strategy. Risk escalation involves passing the risk to the right owner, in this case, the program manager, to ensure that it is recognized, understood, and managed appropriately. Avoiding the risk means eliminating the threat or protecting the project from its impact. Risk mitigating implies decreasing the threat probability of occurrence and/or impact. And finally, transferring the risk entails shifting the threat ownership and responsibility to a third party which may involve payment of a risk premium to the third party assuming the threat.

Question 31 = B
Explanation: One of the key assets of effective managers is their ability to actively listen to those around them. In this situation, Sara has to step into her leadership role and offer guidance to her team member who seems to be overwhelmed. If this team member is unable to manage their workload, she should encourage them to prioritize their work to be more efficient. Ultimately, if the member can't keep up with a realistic workload, a personal improvement plan should be put in place, including training if needed. This process should be fully documented. On the other hand, the daily standup is dedicated to sync work between team members and remove any impediments. So, it's not a suitable frame for addressing individual performance issues. A product should have only one backlog, so a separate backlog should not be created for any purpose.

Question 32 = C
Explanation: Earned Value (EV) is the method of measuring how much of the budget should have been spent in view of the work realized to date. This technique allows the project manager to calculate the Cost Variance (CV), which is the difference between the budgeted cost of the performed work (EV) and its actual cost, to eventually find out whether the project is under or over budget. The

amount of money that has been spent so far represents the Actual Cost (AC).

Question 33 = D
Explanation: An Agile retrospective meeting that takes place at the end of each iteration in which the team discusses what happened during the iteration and determines improvement areas for future iterations. The retrospective allows issues to be identified and discussed along with ideas for improvements. Retrospectives are a primary tool to manage project knowledge and develop the team through discussions of what went well and what needs to be improved.

Question 34 = B
Explanation: It's essential for both the project manager and their team to create selection criteria to rate and score proposals from the suppliers. In the case of a bid or quote, the evaluation criterion is essentially based on the price offered by the seller. In other cases involving proposals, the evaluation criteria can cover various aspects such as the seller experience, references, certifications, etc. In this scenario, Grace has received proposals, so a make-or-buy analysis should have been already carried out. An audit or a performance review should take place at a later stage to verify that all procurement processes were respected and that the purchased items conform to requirements.

Question 35 = A
Explanation: Weighting System is a method for quantifying qualitative data, which is often used to minimize any personal prejudice or judgment effect on the process of source selection. This method works as follows: the project manager assigns a numerical weight to each of the evaluation criteria, then rates the potential sellers according to each criterion. Next, they multiply the weight by rating and calculating the total of the resultant products to finally

get an overall score for each seller. The weighing system method guarantees the award of the contract to the best seller. A screening system is usually used to short-list vendors based on predefined go/no-go criteria. A selecting system is a made-up term.

Question 36 = C
Explanation: Velocity refers to a Scrum development team rate of delivering business value. An agile team's velocity is calculated by simply adding up the estimates or story points of all the features, user stories, requirements, or tasks successfully delivered by all team members during an iteration.

Question 37 = A
Explanation: The term "impediment" refers to problems and issues that stop the project team's progress. Impediments should be constantly and regularly identified as they can hinder a project's completion. Identifying, tracking, and helping remove impediments is one of the main responsibilities of a Project Manager or a Scrum Master. Often, team members are able to remove their own impediments, such as technical issues or risks. However, some impediments involving external issues or risks can be beyond the team's ability to remove them. In such a case, opting for support from outside of the Team is needed to handle impediments.

Question 38 = A
Explanation: When the project is likely to deviate from the planned scope, schedule, cost, or quality requirements, preventive actions must be taken. Such actions are based on a variance and trend analysis and they're proactive in nature. Corrective actions, however, are reactive and are taken in order to bring the project performance back to the baseline when the project has already deviated from the scope, schedule, cost, or quality plan. Defect repair is implemented to adjust a nonconforming product or component. A change request, on the other hand, can be a

corrective action, a preventive action, or even a defect repair (PMBOK 6th edition, page 96).

Question 39 = D
Explanation: The Why Why diagram, known also as Cause and effect diagrams, fishbone diagrams, or Ishikawa diagrams, helps to determine the primary or root cause of the problem by breaking down the causes of the problem into distinct branches. (PMBOK 6th edition, page 293).

Question 40 = B
Explanation: The sum of all tasks is 32 story points. So, it will take 3.2 iterations to complete the work in the given release (32 story points / 10 story points = 3.2 iterations). Since the timebox of an iteration should not be changed, 4 iterations are needed to complete the release tasks.

Question 41 = B
Explanation: A Project Kick-Off Meeting is considered as the formal announcement that the project has been planned and approved for execution. The kick-off meeting takes place at the beginning of the project, once the plan and the project itself get approved but before executing or starting any work. The Project Kick-Off Meeting is usually attended by the sponsor, other managers, project team, and contractors and vendors (Source: Effective Project Management Traditional, Agile, Extreme, Hybrid by Robert K. Wysocki Pages 272, 273). The sprint planning meeting can't be the correct answer for the given situation because outside stakeholders, such as key contactors and stakeholders, are not usually attendees of this meeting. The status meeting, on the other hand, is used to track project progress, when execution has already started. And finally, the scoping meeting is used to define the deliverables of the project, which in this case, should have already taken place since the

tournament has been planned and approved for execution as mentioned.

Question 42 = C
Explanation: A story point is a metric used in estimating the difficulty of a given user story implementation in an agile project. In other words, it is an abstract measure of the effort required to implement a user story. A story point is simply a number that indicates the difficulty level of the story. The difficulty varies depending on the complexities, risks, and efforts involved.

Question 43 = A
Explanation: Parkinson's Law states that "Work expands to fill the time available for its completion" (PMBOK 6th edition, page 197). Student Syndrome, or procrastination, is when people start to apply themselves only at the last minute before a deadline.

Question 44 = B
Explanation: Fixed Price Incentive Fee (FPIF) is a Fixed-price contract. A price limit is determined and set under this contract form, while any other costs above the price ceiling are considered as the seller's liability. All of the other options are types of cost-reimbursable contracts (PMBOK 6th edition, pages 471, 742).

Question 45 = D
Explanation: When the project is closed or terminated due to any reason, you should start the close process. Procurement closure is part of the "Close project" process. The situation in the question requires the project termination, so the best answer is to execute the process that addresses the situation. Also, there is no indication in the question that the project has procurements.

Question 46 = B

Explanation: During the sprint retrospective meeting, all the good and bad aspects of the sprint are discussed. The retrospective meeting is considered as a meeting for improvement, as it is mainly held to find the proper ways and means of identifying potential pitfalls, past errors, and to seek out new ways to avoid those mistakes. This meeting isn't held at the end of the project's last sprint, i.e., it recurrently takes place after the Sprint Review and before the following Sprint Planning. Backlog refinement meeting is used to refine product backlog items. The sprint planning meeting is used to define and evaluate the work of the next sprint.

Question 47 = B
Explanation: First and foremost, Sacha should be proactive and try to manage the conflict between the quality control team and the vendor to work out a solution. If this doesn't work, and the conflict still continues to exist, Sacha should consider other options including taking disciplinary actions or even terminating the contract to avoid potential future damage. Raising the issue to the sponsor is not an appropriate course of action since it's the project manager's responsibility to deal with conflicts and problems encountered throughout the project. Yet, an exception can be made when the decision is beyond the project manager's authority and power, which is not the case here.

Question 48 = B, C
Explanation: In a risk audit, the risk management effectiveness and whether you are following the correct procedures are checked; risk audits look backward to what has occurred. On the other hand, in the risk review, you examine the effectiveness of the risk management plan to reevaluate the risk environment, the risk events, and their relative probability and impact (PMBOK 6th edition, pages 456, 457).

Question 49 = C

Explanation: Management reserve involves the dedicated budget or time reserve for handling unidentified risks or unknown-unknowns (unknown = unidentified, unknowns = risks). This type of reserve is not a calculated budget and does not take part in the cost baseline. Therefore, anytime an unknown risk occurs, the project manager will need permission to use this reserve. On the other hand, a contingency reserve is used for identified risks with predetermined risk response strategies, aka known-unknowns (known = identified, Unknowns = risks).

Question 50 = B
Explanation: Planning activities in an adaptive life cycle entails progressively elaborating the work scope based on the stakeholders' continuous feedback. The project is split into iterations, and at the end of each iteration, the customer reviews the accomplished work on the product. Then, the customer's feedback is used to define the detailed scope of the next iteration. Defining all iterations' work before the start of the project depicts an iterative lifecycle while implementing activities described in the statement of work depicts a predictive life cycle.

Domain 3 (Business environment)

Question 1
Joseph is a project manager. After 8 years in this position, his superiors thought it's time to promote him to a portfolio manager role. A portfolio is:
- **A.** A number of projects, programs, or operations all managed as a collection with the aim to achieve the organization's strategic goals
- **B.** Analyzing IT requirements and ensuring regulatory requirements are followed
- **C.** Following methods, processes, and tools to ensure that projects are managed as designed
- **D.** Creates a common vision and helps senior management to see the potential strategic implications of corporate decisions

Question 2
Charlotte is a junior marketing consultant aspiring to be a project manager. However, she often gets confused about what project management involves. As a project manager yourself and to help Charlotte out, you tell her that project management is:
- **A.** An undertaken temporary endeavor to create a unique service, product, or result
- **B.** The application of a set of knowledge, skills, tools, and techniques to project activities to meet the project requirements
- **C.** The collection of programs that have been grouped to achieve strategic business goals
- **D.** An organizational structure that aims to standardize project-related governance processes

Question 3

Victor performs a cost-benefit analysis before embarking on a new project to assess its potential costs and revenues. The analysis' findings will assess whether the project is profitable or whether the organization should choose another project. Victor finds out that the project's Benefit-Cost Ratio is 1.3. What does this signify?

A. The project's revenue is 1.3 times its profit
B. The project's cost is 1.3 times its profit
C. The project's profit is 1.3 times its cost
D. The project's revenue is 1.3 times its cost

Question 4

In a weak matrix organization, employees work across multiple projects and with various departments within the company to increase employee interaction and promote teamwork spirit. In the event that additional employees are needed, who is in charge of the hiring process under this matrix?

A. The project manager
B. The sponsor
C. The project team
D. The functional manager

Question 5

Debra is a senior software engineer. Recently, she's been assigned to manage a project using the Agile approach. To ensure that she successfully delivers the project, Debra should first:

A. Identify all risks
B. Determine all of the sprints' activities
C. Identify the project success criteria
D. Define quality metrics

Question 6

In order to ensure that the project is performed in accordance with the organization's requirements, Emma, the project manager, opts for a Tailoring process. Under this context, Tailoring is:

A. The knowledge and practices which are applicable to most projects in most cases

B. The application of a set of knowledge, skills, tools, and techniques to the project activities in order to meet its requirements

C. The selection of the appropriate processes, inputs, tools, techniques, and life cycle phases for managing a project

D. The application of knowledge, skills, tools, and techniques needed for meeting a program requirements

Question 7

You notice that certain members of your team confuse projects and operations and oftentimes consider operations to be ongoing projects. You explain to them that there's no such thing as an ongoing project, making sure that you emphasize the difference between project and operations by defining operations as:

A. An undertaken temporary endeavor with the aim of making a distinctive product, service, or result

B. The application of a set of skills, knowledge, tools, and techniques in a project to meet its requirements

C. A collection of programs that have been grouped to achieve strategic business goals

D. Ongoing endeavors that generate repetitive outputs

Question 8

Nancy is attending a meeting to present her project to the company committee for approval. The committee members, including senior managers and subject matter experts, are asking Nancy tough and critical questions. Which project selection technique is the committee using?

A. Brainstorming

B. Scoring model

C. Murder board

D. Benefit analysis

Domain 3 - Answers

Question 1 = A
Explanation: A portfolio is a grouping of projects and programs. A portfolio's purpose is to establish centralized management and oversight for a number of projects and/or programs. It also helps establish standardized governance across the organization. By creating and managing a portfolio, you're ensuring that the organization is choosing the right projects that align with its values, strategies, and goals.

Question 2 = B
Explanation: Project management involves applying a set of processes, skills, knowledge, experience, and methods, to attain a number of predefined project objectives and requirements according to predetermined acceptance criteria.

Question 3 = D
Explanation: A benefit-cost ratio (BCR) is a monetary or qualitative metric that shows the relationship between potential project costs and benefits. If the BCR is greater than 1.0, its revenue will potentially outweigh its cost and if it's less than 1.0, the costs outweigh the gains.
The benefit-cost ratio (BCR) formula is as follows: the sum of the project's benefits divided by the sum of its costs. In this situation, 1.3 means that revenue is 1.3 times the cost. The term "benefit", in the Benefit-Cost Ratio, refers to all the cash flow or income generated from the project, unlike "profit" which represents the net income after deducting all expenses and operating costs.

Question 4 = D
Explanation: The functional manager is the one in charge of managing resources under a weak matrix. This matrix form has a

huge resemblance to a traditional workplace hierarchy. A functional manager is a project's main decision-maker as they supervise all of its aspects. Although the project manager also serves as a point of authority, they primarily report back to the functional manager.

Question 5 = C
Explanation: To ensure the successful delivery of her project, Debra should first identify success criteria with the sponsor. Agreeing upon the project's success criteria will reduce the possibilities of its failure and reinforce its success odds. When setting the project success criteria, you should avoid using unclear and general terms and focus on being precise and clear: e.g., "the product should contain X features", or "the product should be completed by X days".

Question 6 = C
Explanation: Tailoring involves the selection of the appropriate processes, related inputs and outputs, techniques, and life cycle phases in order to manage a project (PMBOK 6th edition, page 2). Project management is the application of a set of knowledge, skills, tools, and techniques to project activities to meet the project requirements. Program management, on the other hand, is the application of knowledge, skills, tools, and techniques to meet the program requirements.

Question 7 = D
Explanation: Operations are ongoing endeavors that produce repetitive outputs. Operations are the continuous execution of activities according to an organization's procedures to produce the same result or a recurrent service. Operations are permanent in nature as they involve all of the common business functions: production, manufacturing, and accounting are examples of operations.

Question 8 = C
Explanation: A murder board is a committee of experts that critically evaluates projects' proposals. In this review, project representatives have to give answers to very critical questions raised by the committee members. It is like an oral exam. The murder board scrutinizes the project by looking for and pointing out reasons why the project should not be considered. The main responsibility of the murder board is to critically and aggressively review the proposed project, while it's the proposer's mission to satisfy each and every query of the board members and prove the worth of the project.

Adaptive approaches/Agile

Question 1
Halfway through the current iteration, the progress report reveals that the agile project you're leading is off track. You didn't expect that since you carefully sequenced and assigned all project work to meet the iteration goal. What should you have done differently to avoid this issue?

    A. Train your team on how to implement the agile approach

    B. Encourage your team to record their progress on the reporting system

    C. Set up a contingency reserve

    D. Encourage your team to self-organize to ensure their buy-in

Question 2
Selma is a project manager at Unique Manufacturing, a company that specializes in creative manufacturing. During a meeting with her project's sponsor, Selma got feedback on the latest prototype and promised to create a revised version accordingly within three weeks. What type of life cycle is Selma using?

    A. Predictive

    B. Incremental

    C. Agile

    D. Iterative

Question 3
A PMO is shifting from a predictive to a more adaptive approach to deliver project outcomes. At an agile training session dedicated to involved employees, an attendee wonders how many individuals should be in a project team. What is the appropriate answer to this?

    A. 1 to 5

    B. 3 to 9

    C. 10 to 15

D. There is no standard number

Question 4
No matter what type of projects he is managing or what type of challenges he might face, Alfred makes sure that his Agile team is always focused on:
   A. Delivering frequently
   B. Planning accurately
   C. Improving quality
   D. Delivering value

Question 5
Vuong was hired as an external agile coach as part of an organization's transformation project. In his final report, he mentioned that measures should be taken to enable agile teams to be cross-functional. What does a cross-functional team mean?
   A. Individuals who collectively determine the best way to accomplish the sprint goal
   B. Individuals who take part in guiding the product direction
   C. Individuals who possess the necessary skills to produce a functioning product
   D. Individuals who are in charge of authorizing and releasing work assignments

Question 6
Sandra is leading an Agile project where the team works in a continuous flow rather than iterations. This approach proved to be less prescriptive and disruptive to her team. Which Agile framework is Sandra using?
   A. Scrum
   B. Adaptive
   C. Incremental
   D. Kanban

Question 7

You are in the stage of selecting a life cycle for your new project. Which of the following reasons will encourage you to choose an adaptive approach over a predictive one?

A. Change requests go through the organization's change control process

B. Change requests are used for frequent planning

C. Change requests are automatically approved

D. Change requests are implemented as soon as they have been received

Question 8

For his new outdoor fitness park project, Umut uses an approach that yields frequent smaller deliverables throughout the span of the project. What type of project life cycle is Umut using?

A. Predictive

B. Incremental

C. Iterative

D. Agile

Question 9

By the end of the third iteration, you delivered the website to your customer and signed a maintenance contract to fix any issues that might occur. On the first day of maintenance, the customer reported an error on the contact page when using a mobile. After verifying with your team, you realize they forgot to test the contact feature on a mobile device. What is this defect called?

A. Primary defect

B. Escaped defect

C. Secondary defect

D. Undetected defect

Question 10

The following chart was presented during a retrospective meeting. Which of the following statements is true regarding this chart?

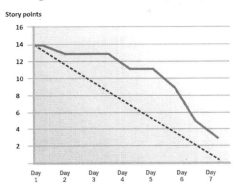

Story points

A. This burnup chart shows that there is work left at the end of the sprint
B. This burnup chart shows that the planned work is completed before the end of the sprint
C. This burndown chart shows that there is work left at the end of the sprint
D. This burndown chart shows that the planned work is completed before the end of the sprint

Question 11
Liam is the scrum master in a project that aims to build a pet training mobile app. During the last retrospective meeting, several topics were evoked. Which of the following topics should be discussed in such a meeting?
A. The feature of tracking a pet's activities
B. Which tasks should be prioritized in the next sprint
C. How to fix the regression of the chat feature
D. Whether the standup timing is suitable for all team members

Question 12

This is Julie's first time managing a project using the scrum framework. One of the team members asked her when a Sprint is considered completed. What should Julie's response be?

A. When all product backlog items are completed

B. When all the tasks in the sprint are completed

C. When the sprint defined timebox ends

D. When all product backlog items meet the Definition of Done (DoD)

Question 13

Idris is facing some challenges because of a key stakeholder. He has collaborated with this stakeholder in previous projects where they frequently changed their requirements and created trouble whenever those requirements were not met. How should Idris manage this stakeholder?

A. Adopt an Agile approach

B. Involve them right from the start

C. Ask them to mend their ways

D. Inform management about it

Question 14

A team, with no defined roles, uses a board and cards to categorize tasks into "To do", "Doing", and "Done". Without too many restrictions, team members grab a card from the "To do" list and begin to work. What agile framework is being described?

A. Scrum

B. Kanban

C. Lean

D. Kaizen

Question 15

Betty is managing a rebranding project using a predictive approach for the planning phase and an Agile approach for the execution phase. She receives an email from one of her key stakeholders requesting an estimation of the project completion date. In order to estimate the completion date, Betty takes into consideration the team's average velocity of 20 story points and the fact that the project still has 205 remaining user story points to complete. How many iterations will it take to finish the project work?

A. 10 iterations

B. 11 iterations

C. 12 iterations

D. Cannot be determined

Question 16

You are managing a software development project. In order to ensure that your agile team is cross-functional, you hire Karen, an experienced designer. A few days later, she informs you that she is unable to do her work properly because the subscription plan of the design application she's using doesn't include all the required functionalities, requesting that her subscription plan be upgraded. What should you do next?

A. Ask her to raise the issue during the next retrospective meeting

B. Tell her to be self-reliant by dealing with the situation and finding turnarounds

C. Explain to her that her subscription plan is sufficient for fulfilling her current tasks

D. Reach out to the appropriate stakeholders to upgrade her subscription plan

Question 17

Using an Agile life cycle, where should product requirements be documented?

A. In the requirements log

B. In the backlog

C. In the team charter

D. In the WBS

Question 18

In a trade show, a prospect stops at the stand of your company, which specializes in selling and installing network security appliances. They ask if your company can provide and set up 10 firewall hardware devices in 5 weeks, recommending an incremental life cycle for delivering 2 firewalls per week. They add that an external security expert will be conducting a penetration test, and that final acceptance will be granted only after all performed cyber attacks are detected and prevented. What is the prospect defining in the above scenario? (Select two)

A. Definition of Done
B. Quality Assurance
C. Technical Requirements
D. Quality Control

Question 19

Tonya is the product owner of an HR solution. To guide the development team on what she intends to achieve, Tonya shares with them the following table depicting the key deliverables of each quarter of the 9-month project. What agile artifact does this represent?

Q1 2021	Q2 2021	Q3 2021
Web App User management Payroll module	Android App Reporting module Dashboard	iOS App Leaves module

A. Product vision statement
B. Product wireframe

C. Product roadmap
D. Product backlog

Question 20
As an experienced scrum master, Olivia is often asked "How long should my team's sprint be?" to which she responds by saying "It depends, you should initially find a balance that works for your team, but typically an agile scrum sprint is _____ long."
  A. 3-5 days
  B. 1 week
  C. 2-4 weeks
  D. 5-8 weeks

Question 21
Taylor is leading a gaming equipment development project. The project team holds a monthly status review meeting with the product owner to review post-iteration deliverables. What's the best communication type to use in a status review meeting?
  A. Push
  B. Pull
  C. Interactive
  D. Formal

Question 22
During the standup meeting, your team member, Abubakar, invokes an impediment he is facing. In order to address this impediment, you suggest that two other members of your team sit with Abubakar and collaborate to find out a solution. What technique are you suggesting? (Select two)
  A. Pairing
  B. Swarming
  C. Mobbing
  D. Brainstorming

Question 23

All of the following are either Agile or Lean frameworks except:

A. Scrumban

B. eXtreme Programming

C. Waterfall

D. Crystal Methods

Question 24

Agile scrum simplifies the project management process by decomposing it into cycles, aka Sprints. As Agile adoption increases, more terminologies, tools, and techniques are introduced and adopted. For instance, Zero Sprint refers to:

A. The preparation step for the first sprint

B. The first sprint of the project

C. A sprint that doesn't have any user stories

D. A sprint where none of the tasks is completed

Question 25

Martin got assigned to lead a new project. Wondering about the project completion date, the product owner asks Martin: "How many story points do you expect to complete per sprint?". In order to provide the product owner with an accurate response, Martin should:

A. Estimate the sprint velocity based on his team members' input

B. Run multiple sprints in order to be able to answer the product owner's question

C. Rely on his own judgment as an experienced project manager to estimate the sprint velocity

D. Engage the team in determining the sprint velocity based on their previous agile projects

Question 26

Throughout her long experience as a project manager, Lily has always followed a servant leadership style, particularly with agile teams. What does servant leadership imply?

A. One individual in charge of directing and guiding the team

B. Carrying out work through iterations, with one prominent leader

C. Naming a team leader, while team members serve as followers

D. Understanding and addressing the needs of team members

Question 27
In order to handle high levels of change and involve ongoing participation of all interested parties, Iden chose for his project a change-driven life cycle which is also known as:

A. Adaptive life cycle

B. Predictive life cycle

C. Waterfall life cycle

D. Hybrid life cycle

Question 28
In projects following the Scrum framework, which of the following questions won't be asked to team members during daily stand-ups?

A. What have you completed since the last stand-up?

B. What will you complete until the next stand-up?

C. What do we need to finish as a team?

D. Are there any impediments?

Question 29
Thomas realized that his team's velocity is fluctuating when reviewing their burn-up chart. While searching for the root cause, he notices that one of his team members has a very slow performance compared to his teammates, which is negatively impacting the whole team's performance. How should Thomas address this issue?

A. Plan training sessions for the team member

B. Acquire a more competent resource

C. Mentor the concerned team member

D. Reassign the team member to another project

Question 30

Edward is managing an e-commerce website project using the Agile approach. After a slow start tensioned with disputes, his team members are starting to get along and support each other's needs. In which area of the Tuckman ladder does Edward's team currently exist?

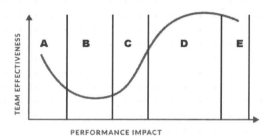

A. Area A

B. Area B

C. Area C

D. Area D

Question 31

You're following an Agile approach to lead a software development project. In order to ensure that your project satisfies customer needs effectively and efficiently, you decided to put into practice some well-known agile quality checking strategies. All of the following are strategies for agile quality checking, except:

A. Milestone review

B. Iteration
C. Dynamic code analysis
D. Daily Standup

Question 32
During the project planning phase, the scrum master, product owner, and cross-functional team members select the backlog items to be executed in the next sprint. In such a team, who commits to delivering business value by the end of the sprint?
A. The cross-functional team
B. The scrum master
C. The product owner
D. The entire Scrum team

Question 33
You have been assigned to manage an agile project that is already mid-execution. Which of the following should you check to examine the high-level description of the project scope?
A. Project charter
B. User stories
C. Epics
D. Work breakdown structure

Question 34
Bella is a project manager within an organization that uses Agile practices. In order to evaluate her project performance, Bella uses (Select two):
A. Cost performance index
B. Value-based measurements
C. Empirical measurements
D. Schedule performance index

Question 35

Wang is leading a web project using an adaptive approach. The project consists of an automatic notification system that alerts users when their cloud expenses exceed a predefined threshold. Wang and his team are currently preparing and updating user stories for the next iterations. What activity is being undertaken?
  A. Backlog refinement
  B. Schedule management
  C. Project management
  D. Sprint review

Question 36
Dalida is managing an organic skincare branding project. When checking the sprint performance, she becomes dissatisfied with the current progress. Meeting with her team to discuss the matter, she learns that some issues were not accurately estimated due to missing key information during the sprint planning. Knowing that Dalida's team uses story points for estimating issues and user stories, how should she address this problem?
  A. Re-estimate all of the sprint's issues and user stories
  B. Reduce or re-estimate the velocity of the sprint
  C. Do nothing and raise the problem in the sprint retrospective
  D. Collaborate with her team to review the remaining issues in the sprint backlog

Question 37
The role of a product owner within an Agile project is:
  A. Coordinating the work of the sprint and running the team
  B. Having a vested interest in the project and its outcomes and interfacing with stakeholders
  C. Representing the business unit, customer, or end-user
  D. Completing the backlog items and signing up tasks based on established priorities

Question 38

For your new project, you decided to create a Work Breakdown Structure (WBS), define and sequence all activities, and then execute tasks in month-long cycles. The sponsor can change 30% of the subsequent cycle's scope of work with no need for a change request. Which of the following project life cycles is being implemented?

    A. Adaptive
    B. Hybrid
    C. Predictive
    D. Iterative

Question 39

One of the challenges faced by organizations when they shift to Agile ways of working is the often-mentioned need to build teams made up of "T-shaped" people. A "T" shaped person is:

    A. A generalist who is able to tackle any task within the backlog, regardless of the required skills
    B. A person who had freshly started their career and needs coaching by the scrum master
    C. An individual who specializes in a single field and rarely contributes outside of it
    D. An individual who supplements their competence in one area with less-developed skills in associated areas and have an aptitude for collaboration

Question 40

Ahmed is an Agile consultant. A medium-sized IT company, that had been previously using the predictive approach, asked him to assist in their transition to the Agile approach. Which of the following factors should Ahmed take into consideration when establishing the Agile approach?

    A. The organization familiarity with the predictive approach
    B. The organization's culture
    C. Scrum master's existence

D. The organization's size

Question 41
Amy works as a project manager for a company that is undergoing a reorganization. During a staff meeting, she learns that management has decided to shift technology to use the cloud. Amy uses an Agile approach to manage her project, and since she knows that this shift will have a direct impact on the project, she decides to:
- **A.** Assess the impact with the sponsor before moving forward with the change management procedure
- **B.** Assess the impact with the team and refine the backlog
- **C.** Close the project and start over with a new one that will properly adapt to the new technological transition
- **D.** Send a formal request to the sponsor asking for an exception against using the cloud

Question 42
You are assigned to manage a graphic design project using the scrum framework. Which of the following events will not be used by your team?
- **A.** Sprint planning
- **B.** Weekly scrum
- **C.** Sprint review
- **D.** Sprint retrospective

Question 43
Sophie is managing a software project using the Agile approach. During a meeting with her team, she shows them how much work still needs to be done during the current iteration. What is Sophie showing her team?
- **A.** Schedule
- **B.** Burnup chart
- **C.** Milestone chart
- **D.** Burndown chart

Question 44
Which of the below statements represent the most accurate definition of backlog refinement? (Select three)
   A. The process of creating the initial list of product requirements formerly known as backlog grooming.
   B. When the product owner or team members review the backlog to make sure it has the proper items
   C. The continuous elaboration of project requirements to satisfy the stakeholders' needs
   D. The continuous activity of writing, updating, and prioritizing requirements

Question 45
You are leading an internal accounting software development project. During a sprint planning meeting, you tackle a task that involves setting an automatic email as a reminder when unpaid invoices miss the due dates. Your Agile team agrees to assign the task a total of 8 Story Points, based on the developers' estimate of 5 story points and the testers' estimate of 3 points. Which of the following statements is correct regarding this situation?
   A. The project manager should be the one to allocate points, not the team
   B. Points should be allocated for the whole task, not for its segments
   C. Story points should never be estimated, they should be determined instead
   D. The team should ask the relevant stakeholders about the estimate

Question 46
Jack is managing a two-year project involving a lot of uncertainty and unforeseen complexity. His team expects adjustments as the scope of work gradually becomes clearer over time. To set

expectations right with stakeholders, what should Jack clear up concerning his choice of using an iterative approach to manage the project?

    A. That work will be subject to short feedback loops with the backlog being reprioritized in each iteration

    B. That work will be developed progressively based on monthly feedback loops

    C. That all tasks will be prioritized upfront, and that work will be gradually decomposed

    D. That the team will start executing work from the backlog bottom-up

Question 47

A project manager needs to choose the appropriate project management approach for the project they're leading. There are a variety of approaches to choose from, each ideally suited for a specific project type. Agile and Scrum are two of the most common and often conflated terms. Given their similarities, they can get confusing sometimes, but they are, in fact, two distinct concepts. What is the primary distinction between Scrum and Agile?

    A. Agile is a set of values and principles, while Scrum only presents a set of values.

    B. Agile is a set of values, principles, and practices, while Scrum involves only a set of values and principles.

    C. Agile is a set of values and principles, while Scrum represents a set of values, principles, and practices.

    D. Agile is a framework, while Scrum is a philosophy.

Question 48

The traditional format of a daily stand-up is to gather in a circle near the relevant task board and each member takes his turn to answer a set of questions. Which of the statements below explains the meaning of daily stand-up in agile?

    A. It is a meeting where the upcoming work schedule is discussed

B. It is a meeting during which the team is asked about what they did on the previous day and their plan for the current day along with any problems they faced during the execution of their tasks

C. It is a daily brainstorming session

D. It is a daily lessons learned session

Question 49

Agile is not fit for all projects, despite all the advantages it can bring forth. Therefore, it's important to understand the drawbacks of this approach. Which of the options below are disadvantages of the Agile approach? (Select three)

A. Poor resource planning

B. Limited documentation

C. Self-organized teams

D. Fragmented output

Question 50

The Sprint goals were not met by your Scrum team. A key team member took two days off at the start of the four-week Sprint due to a family emergency. What is the most likely reason for the team's failure to achieve the Sprint goals?

A. You didn't assign a replacement for the OOTO (Out Of The Office) member

B. Your team is inexperienced

C. Your team did not plan the sprint effectively

D. Your team is overworked

Adaptive approaches/Agile - Answers

Question 1 = D
Explanation: As the project manager of an Agile project, rather than sequencing and assigning work yourself, you should empower your team as a whole to be self-organized through handling iteration tasks selection and prioritization. This will ensure a high level of buy-in from your team. Self-organized teams typically result in a highly motivated staff since it allows them to gain the autonomy to choose the most efficient way to accomplish their work. Self-organizing teams are neither directed nor controlled by others outside the team.

Question 2 = D
Explanation: Iterative life cycles use successive prototypes or Proofs of Concept (PoC). Activities are repeated in cycles to produce more information and ideas to improve the product. In this scenario, Selma's project involves a single delivery rather than a series of smaller deliveries. For this reason, incremental and agile life cycles should be eliminated (Agile practice Guide, page 18).

Question 3 = B
Explanation: An Agile team recommended size is 3 to 9 members. Since the level of communication deteriorates as a team's size increases, Agile organizations favor smaller teams. For instance, it's better to have two teams of five people than one team of ten.

Question 4 = D
Explanation: Delivering value should always be an agile team's top priority as it represents one of the agile manifesto principles: "working software over comprehensive documentation". From the client's perspective, value represents the benefit derived from using a product or a service.

Question 5 = C
Explanation: A cross-functional team must possess the necessary competencies for creating a product or a service independently, without relying on other members outside of the team. On the other hand, a self-organizing team is when individuals collectively determine the best way to accomplish the sprint goal.

Question 6 = D
Explanation: The Kanban method involves pulling work into the system only when the team is capable of handling it. The Kanban method prioritizes productivity and efficiency through its workflow approach. Unlike the Scrum team, a Kanban team does not have predefined roles.

Question 7 = B
Explanation: Unlike the predictive life cycle which requires change requests to go through the organization's change control process, the adaptive life cycle welcomes changes and uses them for frequent planning. During each iteration, the team focuses on producing a subset of the product's features, while continuously refining and reprioritizing the product backlog items to meet new or modified requirements. This means that change requests are not automatically approved; instead, they are discussed with the product owner first, and then they get prioritized in subsequent iterations as per their recommendations.

Question 8 = B
Explanation: Incremental life cycles focus on speed of delivery. In this type of life cycle, the project is divided into increments which are successively delivered to avoid waiting for everything to be completed in order to create a solution. In this scenario, Umut didn't ask for feedback to adjust deliverables. Hence, the iterative

life cycle can't be the correct answer. Since Agile = incremental + iterative, then Agile can't be the right answer either.

Question 9 = B
Explanation: An escaped defect is one that was not detected by the project team but rather discovered by the customer or end-user after the product is released. All other options are made-up terms.

Question 10 = C
Explanation: This chart is a burndown chart that shows that there is work left at the end of the sprint. In fact, 3 story points are left to be completed in order to finalize all the planned work for the exhibited 7-day sprint.

Question 11 = D
Explanation: During the sprint retrospective, Liam should identify what went well during the sprint and what can be done differently in the next sprint. A possible topic is the timing of the standup. If team members are showing dissatisfaction with its current schedule, then the retrospective meeting is the right event to discuss the issue. Backlog refinement meetings should address topics like the feature of tracking a pet's activities or how to fix the regression of the chat feature. On the other hand, the sprint planning meeting is the right meeting for discussing which tasks should be prioritized in the next sprint.

Question 12 = C
Explanation: A sprint is considered complete only when it reaches the end of its duration/timebox, which is usually 1 to 4 weeks. In some cases, the sprint ends without finishing all of the assigned tasks, so this can't be the criteria for sprint completion.

Question 13 = B

Explanation: Idris should involve his key stakeholder at the very beginning of the project to help reduce and uncover risks, as well as increase their "buy-in." While implementing an agile approach may benefit Idris, it does not address the issue of stakeholder management. If the question were "what's the appropriate life cycle for Idris' project?", then adopting an agile approach would be the right answer.

Question 14 = B
Explanation: Kanban is an agile method that employs a pull-based work system where tasks are assigned only when resources are available. Unlike Scrum, the Kanban team has no formal roles. Additionally, Kanban practice has fewer restrictions than Scrum. Lean is not an agile framework. In contrast, agile and kanban are subsets of lean (Agile Practice Guide, page 11). Kaizen is a quality and resource management philosophy of applying continuous small improvements to increase productivity and reduce costs.

Question 15 = B
Explanation: If the team maintains an average velocity of 20 story points per iteration, it would take 11 iterations to complete the remaining 205 story points. (205 story points / 20 story points = 10.25 iterations). Since you should not change the timebox of an iteration, you'll need 11 iterations to complete the work.

Question 16 = D
Explanation: As a servant leader, you should reach out to the appropriate stakeholder in order to upgrade Karen's subscription plan. In an agile work environment, the project manager should listen to the impediments faced by their team members and act to solve them. If Karen's subscription plan cannot be upgraded, then you should explain this to her, asking her to try finding turnarounds, such as using other complementary applications that offer the functionalities that her current application is missing.

Agile teams are self-organized, i.e they decide how they should perform their work. Thus, forcing Karen to use a limited subscription plan is inappropriate. Furthermore, since Karen is an experienced designer, she is able to clearly identify her needs, therefore the scrum master or the project manager should cater to her job requirements rather than argue with her. Retrospective meetings are set up to improve processes and not to remove impediments.

Question 17 = B
Explanation: Project requirements are documented under the backlog as user stories. The backlog user stories are then continuously prioritized and refined. The WBS is only used in the predictive life cycle.

Question 18 = A, D
Explanation: A Definition of Done (DoD) is a checklist of the required criteria for considering a product ready for delivery (Agile Practice Guide, page 151). Furthermore, the prospect is setting a quality control process that focuses on defect identification. Quality assurance, on the other hand, focuses on defect prevention. Technical requirements cover the product requirements, such as WiFi support, storage, number of LANs, etc.

Question 19 = C
Explanation: The product roadmap is built by the product owner to demonstrate the anticipated sequence of deliverables over the project duration (Agile Practice Guide, page 52). As an Agile artifact, the product roadmap sets the product's strategic view, indicating where the product is headed in both short and long terms. In agile organizations, the product roadmap serves as a guide rather than a project plan. The product roadmap is different from the product backlog in that the product roadmap provides the big picture while the product backlog tackles the practical and feasible steps

required to tangibly create the product. The Product wireframe is a mockup or a sketch of the user interface, high-level functionality, page layout, etc. A product vision statement outlines what a product would look like to ultimately achieve its vision and give purpose to its existence. A vision statement should be short, simple, and specific.

Question 20 = C
Explanation: A Sprint has to be long enough for the team to finish all included stories. As per a Scrum rule, a Sprint should never exceed one month. The duration of a sprint depends on the project size and complexity as well as the team's capacities. It takes 2 to 4 weeks on average to complete a sprint with a team of 3-9 members working on a single project.

Question 21 = C
Explanation: When an immediate response is required and the information you're communicating is sensitive and could be misinterpreted, you should use interactive communication. It involves one or more people sharing thoughts and ideas, with participants responding in real-time. Interactive communication can take place through teleconferences or face-to-face contact. When using communication media such as emails, the project manager can't pick up on stakeholders' facial expressions and body language.

Question 22 = B, C
Explanation: With swarming and mobbing, multiple team members or the entire team focus collectively on resolving a specific impediment. While pairing, swarming and mobbing are collaboration techniques used by the Agile team (Agile Practice Guide, page 39), the situation doesn't describe pairing since this technique requires only two team members to work together to

resolve an issue. Brainstorming, on the other hand, is used to generate ideas, rather than to resolve issues.

Question 23 = C
Explanation: Waterfall is a predictive methodology that was deemed too rigid to handle the changing requirements brought on by new technology or a demanding client. Even though there are numerous Agile and Lean frameworks, the Agile Practice Guide only addresses Scrum, Kanban Method, Scrumban, eXtreme Programming (XP), Crystal Methods, Dynamic Systems Development Method (DSDM), Feature-Driven Development (FDD), and Agile Unified Process.

Question 24 = A
Explanation: The term "Zero sprint" refers to a step in the process of preparing the initial sprint. Before initiating a project, various activities must be completed, which are all referred to as the Zero sprint. Doing preliminary research, deciding on technical choices, and preparing for backlogs are all examples of activities performed prior to project launch. Mike Cohn illustrated the usage of Sprint 0 in his book "Succeeding with Agile Software Development Using Scrum" (Page 152).

Question 25 = D
Explanation: Typically, you should rely on the available historical data of your team velocity in order to set a reasonable and achievable number of story points per sprint, depending entirely on your team capacities and how much they can accomplish. When a new team has no historical data, the sprint forecast can be done based on your experience with similar projects along with collaborative estimations from the entire team, to determine how many story points they can potentially deliver in the first sprint.

Question 26 = D

Explanation: According to the Agile Practice Guide, servant leadership implies leading your team through focusing on understanding and addressing their needs to yield the best performance possible (Agile Practice Guide, page 33).

Question 27 = A
Explanation: A change-driven life cycle is also referred to as an Agile, adaptive, flexible, or change-focused life cycle. This life cycle is characterized by the ability to react and adapt to high levels of change as well as the constant involvement and participation of different parties. On the other hand, a waterfall or predictive life cycle is sequential and rigid. Hybrid is a combination of predictive and adaptive life cycles.

Question 28 = C
Explanation: In contrast to flow-based Agile which focuses on the team's throughput, iteration-based Agile focuses on accountability through three standard questions:
- What was completed yesterday?
- What will be completed today?
- Are there any blockers or impediments?

Question 29 = C
Explanation: When a team member's performance is negatively impacting the project progress, the project manager should interfere immediately. Since training the team member would take time, mentoring them would be a more suitable option for this urgent issue. Mentoring can help the team member enhance their performance. It's among the project manager's responsibilities to serve as a guide in identifying and assisting their team members with their learning needs to ensure better functioning and performance. By offering enough support and attention, the team member will respond positively by working harder, which will naturally result in better functioning and performance. A mentor

should however continue to observe the team member's performance and provide feedback to help them refine and improve their work.

Question 30 = C
Explanation: Getting over the storming stage (area B) means that the team has managed to resolve their conflicts and that a sense of unity is shaped. During the norming phase (area C), a sense of cohesion and unity emerges, a common consensus is developed, and personal differences start to diminish. Team performance is improved at this point as members get more goal-oriented. However, if disagreements resurface, the team can slide back into the storming phase. Please note that on the real PMP exam you may be asked to answer this type of question by clicking on the correct area in the image.

Question 31 = D
Explanation: Daily stand-up is not used as an agile quality strategy, it is rather a daily meeting for work status control. For agile quality checking, iterations, dynamic code analysis, and milestones review are commonly used strategies.
1. The Iterative strategy allows constant adjustments, refinement, and work review to incrementally improve team performance, thus permitting continuous assessment and optimization of the implemented development processes.
2. The dynamic code analysis process consists of various steps including; preparing input data, running a test program, and analyzing the output data.
3. Milestone reviews represent formal reviews pre-set during project planning. Milestone reviews are carried out to assess performance and progress over a specific time span (or milestone) in comparison to the plan's set goals.

Question 32 = A

Explanation: When sprint planning is complete, the cross-functional team members finalize their commitment to the business value that will be delivered by the end of the sprint. The sprint goal and the selected product backlog items embody this commitment (Essential Scrum a practical guide to the most popular agile process by Rubin, Kenneth S, page 346). On the other hand, the product owner owns the product backlog items. Keep in mind that the Product Backlog represents work that needs to be done to create the entire product, while the Sprint backlog is a subset that represents the work that needs to be executed in the current sprint.

Question 33 = A
Explanation: You should refer to the project charter to find a 'high-level description' of the project. The project charter is a formal document that describes your project in its entirety, including its objectives, work processes, and stakeholders. This is a project planning document that can be used throughout the whole project lifecycle. User stories and epics only represent the detailed requirements, not the entire high-level description of the project scope. The Work Breakdown Structure (WBS) also outlines the detailed requirements of projects that follow a predictive life cycle.

Question 34 = B, C
Explanation: Agile favors empirical and value-based measurements instead of predictive measurements (Agile Practice Guide, page 61). Agile teams focus on measuring value and implementing an empirical process where progress is based on observations of reality, facts, experiences, and evidence. The Agile approach consists of a fixed cost and schedule, hence CPI & SPI couldn't be used.

Question 35 = A
Explanation: Backlog refinement involves preparing the next iteration's stories. In order to ensure the backlog contains the right

items for the next iteration, the project manager, along with their team, reviews and prioritizes backlog items, making sure that top items are ready to be delivered. This activity can take place as a formal planned meeting or as a regular ongoing task.

Question 36 = D
Explanation: A team should ideally prepare all of the sprint issues and user stories before its start date. However, this is not always the case for a number of reasons. Inaccurate story estimations can result in unsatisfying progress and unfinished tasks in the Sprint Backlog. In this case, you should collaborate with your team to review and complete the remaining Sprint issues. You should first identify the issues that your team didn't finish, document them, and determine the needed effort for accomplishing them. In a second step, you adjust priorities, re-estimate issues, and reflect on what happened in the sprint retrospective.

Question 37 = C
Explanation: The product owner represents the stakeholders and is regarded as the voice of the customer. The Product Owner is responsible for maximizing the value produced by the team and ensuring stories meet the user's needs and comply with the definition of "Done". Apart from the project team, this position has significant relationships and obligations, including working with upper management, end-users, and other stakeholders.

Question 38 = B
Explanation: Hybrid life cycles incorporate different components from various life cycles. In the described scenario, you are combining predictive (by planning everything at the beginning of the project), with iterative (by executing work in cycles), and adaptive life cycles (by allowing a 30% change without going through a formal process).

Question 39 = D
Explanation: "T" shaped people typically have encompassing expertise in one field with supporting but less-developed skills in related areas. T-shaped people also have an aptitude for collaboration. "I" shaped people, on the other hand, have a profound specialization in one domain and only seldom participate in work outside of that domain (Agile Practice Guide, Page 42).

Question 40 = B
Explanation: An organization's culture influences the type of project management approaches adopted by project teams. The knowledge of existing approaches, the size of the organization, and the competency of its team are all factors that contribute to the culture.

Question 41 = B
Explanation: Agile practices provide the ability to adapt quickly to new conditions. In this case, changing requirements would impose conducting an assessment and refinement of the backlog with the team's assistance.

Question 42 = B
Explanation: Scrum teams employ four main events: sprint planning, daily scrum, sprint review, and sprint retrospective.

Question 43 = D
Explanation: Unlike the burnup chart which shows completed work, a burndown chart is a graphical depiction of work left to do against time (Agile Practice Guide, pages 62-63).

Question 44 = B, C, D
Explanation: Backlog refinement (formerly referred to as backlog grooming) occurs when the product owner along with some, or all of the team members check the backlog to make sure it contains the

proper items, that they are prioritized, and that the ones at the top are ready to be delivered. This activity occurs regularly and can be either an officially scheduled meeting or an ongoing activity. The process of developing the initial list of product requirements represents backlog elaboration or creation.

Question 45 = B
Explanation: Story points are assigned to each story to estimate the total effort involved in bringing a feature or functionality to life. Thus, they shouldn't be assigned partially. The team has to carefully consider how much work and effort is involved in each story to ensure that they can deliver on the work they've committed to.

Question 46 = A
Explanation: Short feedback loops and backlog reprioritization are common in projects that use an iterative approach for the project life cycle. Frequent delivery and feedback permit the team to prioritize and respond to changes more efficiently. The duration of the iteration should be adjusted according to the project's characteristics. For example, a monthly feedback loop could not be appropriate for a two-month-long project. Weekly or fortnightly feedback will be more convenient in this case.

Question 47 = C
Explanation: On the surface, Agile and Scrum look similar as they both rely on an iterative process, frequent client interaction, and collaborative decision-making. The primary distinction between Agile and Scrum is that Agile is a project management philosophy that utilizes a core set of values or principles, while Scrum is a specific Agile practice used to facilitate a project. Although Scrum is an approach within Agile, Agile does not necessarily imply Scrum since Agile encompasses a wide range of approaches. Scrum is based on a small set of core values, principles, and practices

(collectively forming the Scrum framework). References: Agile Alliance & Essential Scrum a practical guide to the most popular agile process by Rubin, Kenneth S (Preface).

Question 48 = B
Explanation: Daily standup is a meeting held by members of the project team. A daily stand-up meeting is intended to bring the team together for a status update, to ensure that everyone is on the same page and has insight into what is going on, whether it's good or bad. Such a meeting usually takes up to 15 minutes during which every team member is asked three questions: What did you do yesterday that helped your team meet the Sprint Goal? What will you do today to help your Team meet the Sprint Goal? And, Did you face any impediments that prevented you or your team from meeting the Sprint Goal?

Question 49 = A, B, D
Explanation: Poor resource planning, limited documentation, and fragmented output are three key downsides of the agile approach. Since Agile is built on the premise that teams don't know what their final result will look like earlier on the project, it's difficult to anticipate project costs, time, and resources at the start, and this difficulty becomes more pronounced as projects become larger and more complex. Moreover, in Agile, documentation occurs during the project, and it is often done "just in time", rather than at the beginning of the project. As a consequence, documentation becomes less informative. Additionally, while incremental delivery can help launch goods faster, it's often regarded as one of the Agile approach disadvantages: when teams work on each component at different time periods, the end result often becomes fragmented instead of being one coherent deliverable. On the other hand, Agile is based on self-organizing teams who are proven to have higher velocity, increased quality, and less need for team management.

Question 50 = C

Explanation: When a team struggles to achieve the sprint goals, it's mainly due to poor sprint planning. A team that fails to reach its sprint target is a team that can't properly plan its work, does not have a clear understanding of its own capabilities, or does not have a good sense of how to forecast stories and/or tasks. A team member's two days off should not be an excuse for missing the sprint goals.

Predictive approach

Question 1

Network diagrams are a visual display of project work as they show the connection between work activities and how they progress from the project start to its completion. The longest path in a network diagram is known as:

   A. Critical Path
   B. Critical Chain
   C. Float
   D. Free Float

Question 2

In an interior design project for a library, the client asks the team to increase the number of bookshelves beyond what was agreed on. Since the project is on schedule and adding additional shelves will make no difference, the project manager consents to the client's request. This is an example of?

   A. Gold Plating
   B. Customer Obsession
   C. Scope Creep
   D. Successful Project

Question 3

You are managing a software development project using the predictive approach. A day prior to the release deadline, Finn, a quality engineer in your team, discovered a bug that may induce a one-week delay. What should you do next?

   A. Inform the stakeholders that there is a bug that requires 2 or 3 days to fix and put more pressure on the engineers to fix it on time
   B. Meet with stakeholders and inform them about the situation and that it may take a week to resolve the bug

C. Update the lessons learned and add them to your organizational process assets

D. Create and send a change request document to the change control board

Question 4

Anna is a project manager for Massive Fun, a company specialized in eco-friendly kids' toys. Two months into the project, she launches the second phase consisting in developing biodegradable playing dough. Hence, she meets with her sponsor to check if any potential players were left out in the first phase and to discuss these new stakeholders' influence. The activity that Anna is carrying out along with her sponsor can be identified as:

A. Planning stakeholder engagement

B. Identifying stakeholders

C. Planning resource management

D. Identifying risks

Question 5

Dany is leading a project to implement a new ERP system for a local customer. She guides the project team to define the project requirements in detail before moving to execution. The project will be delivered after 4 months, but the customer will pay Dany's organization in monthly installments. Which of the following project life cycles is Dany adopting?

A. Predictive

B. Adaptive

C. Iterative

D. Incremental

Question 6

Clyde is managing a 12-month project with a budget of $100,000. Six months have passed and $60,000 has been spent. On closer inspection, Clyde finds out that so far, only 40% of the work has been completed. The value of the completed 40% work is referred to as:

   A. Planned value
   B. Earned value
   C. Actual cost
   D. Cost variance

Question 7
Alyssa is carrying out the initial planning activities for a gas pipeline construction project using a predictive approach. When estimating the "install pipeline" activity, one team member states that they ran the same length of pipes in 14 hours on a previous similar project. Another team member claims that they can run 100 meters of gas pipes per hour. The team will need to run a total of 1000 meters of pipes. Using the analogous estimating technique, how many hours will it take the team to run the gas pipeline?

   A. 10
   B. 11
   C. 12
   D. 14

Question 8
During project execution, a team member reaches out to the project manager to inquire about the work she needs to accomplish in this phase of the project. Which of these documents comprises thorough descriptions of work packages?

   A. WBS
   B. WBS Dictionary
   C. Activity List
   D. Scope management plan

Question 9
An activity has an early start (ES) of day 5, a late start (LS) of day 12, an early finish (EF) of day 10, and a late finish (LF) of day 17.

Which of the following statements are correct regarding this activity? (Select two)

A. The activity is on the critical path
B. The activity is not on the critical path
C. The activity has a float
D. The activity has a lag

Question 10

Dave manages a construction project. Throughout its execution, his project was influenced by both Enterprise Environmental Factors and Organizational Process Assets. Match the following statements with the corresponding influence category:

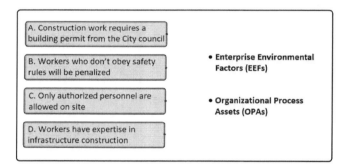

Question 11

The project team cannot plan for risks that are believed to be difficult to find or imagine. Therefore, a _____ reserve should be set for threats that were not identified in advance.

A. Management
B. Buffer
C. Contingency
D. Additional

Question 12

In a predictive approach, which of the following statements are true about project deliverables? (Select two)

  A. Project deliverables should be identified throughout the project lifecycle
  B. Project deliverables can be products, services, or any other type of outcome
  C. Once project deliverables have been identified, they should not be changed anymore
  D. The acceptance criteria for deliverables should be described in the project agreement

Question 13

For a museum construction project, concrete is poured after the completion of rebar and formwork. Workers must now wait 14 days before removing the formwork, as the concrete strength must be sufficient for this operation. The 14 days are an example of:

  A. A Lead
  B. A Lag
  C. Crashing
  D. Fast-tracking

Question 14

A project task is 90% complete. It cannot, however, be finished until another task is completed. What type of dependency is this? (Select two)

  A. Finish-to-start (FS)
  B. Finish-to-finish (FF)
  C. Mandatory dependency
  D. Discretionary dependency

Question 15

Brody is the project manager of a dating mobile app. He received an urgent change request from his client. After checking the change request, Brody realized that implementing it could be very costly. What is the best course of action for him to take?

A. Discuss the cost impact with the client
B. Implement it straight away
C. Reject it due to its cost impact
D. Not allow any change requests regardless of the cost impact

Question 16

The predictive life cycle takes advantage of which of the following characteristics of a project? (Select two)

A. Scope, time, and cost are determined in the early phases of the life cycle
B. Change is limited as much as possible during project execution
C. The scope is determined early in the project life cycle, but time and cost are routinely modified
D. After one iteration, deliverables have enough functionality to be considered complete

Question 17

You are managing a project with a predictive approach. Your project team members have been allocated to your project with 50% availability. However, you recently discovered that they have been spending less than 50% of their time working on your project. Your project schedule is about to become heavily delayed, putting deadlines in jeopardy. What should you do?

A. Discuss getting additional resources with the project sponsor
B. Negotiate clear and written assignments with reliable scheduling priorities with functional managers
C. Adjust the schedule and negotiate new deadlines due to unexpectedly slow work progress
D. Crash the project in order to complete it on time

Question 18

Upon request, Phil presented to his superiors his order of magnitude estimations for the hostel construction project. The level of accuracy for the order of magnitude estimation is:

A. -25% to +75%
B. -25% to +50%
C. -10% to +25%
D. -5% to +10%

Question 19

Within predictive life cycles, which of the following terms is used for both costs and schedules to establish what you'll measure against later in the monitoring and controlling phase?

A. Variance
B. Expected value
C. Baseline
D. Estimates

Question 20

John, who is the only carpenter in the project team, is only available to work part-time. Since his work is on the critical path, the project's planned completion date had to be pushed back to align with John's availability. Such adjustment of the project schedule to handle resource constraints is called:

A. Load Balancing
B. Resource Loading
C. Resource Leveling
D. Resource Smoothing

Question 21

The following diagram represents the decomposition of the project deliverables into smaller tasks. What is this diagram called?

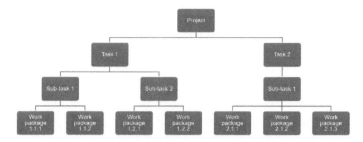

A. Affinity diagram
B. Product breakdown
C. Product roadmap
D. Work breakdown structure

Question 22

Samuel is the manager of a new virtual reality game development project. The project is scheduled to last 10 months with a budget of $100,000. Now, one month has passed by and the project is 10% complete. What is the project's current Schedule Performance Index (SPI)?

    A. 0.1
    B. 1
    C. 1.1
    D. 10

Question 23

Choosing a predictive approach to plan his agriculture project, Joseph uses the _____ method to estimate the cost by using a work breakdown.

    A. Analogous
    B. Parametric
    C. Top-down
    D. Bottom-up

Question 24
You are assigned to manage an industrial project following a predictive approach. During the risk planning phase, you decided to create a contingency reserve for:
   A. Passive acceptance
   B. Active acceptance
   C. Workaround
   D. Unidentified risks

Question 25
You are managing a construction project. Setting up the light spots is pending since ceiling tiles are still being installed, which may cause some delays within your project. What should you refer to in order to check your electricity team's availability in the next two weeks to resolve this dependency?
   A. Resource Calendars
   B. Responsibility Assignment Matrix (RAM)
   C. RACI Matrix
   D. Organigram

Question 26
Upon your organization's request, you created the following high-level hierarchical list of team and physical resources for a project that consists in creating a bulk SMS platform for marketing campaigns. What is this visual representation called?

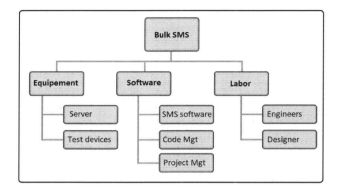

A. Resource calendar
B. Organization breakdown structure
C. Resource breakdown structure
D. RACI chart

Question 27

You are managing a project that has a fixed fee of $5,000 and an estimated cost of $50,000. Knowing that the actual cost of the project reached $60,000, what is the total cost of the Cost-Plus-Fixed-Fee contract?

    A. $50,000
    B. $55,000
    C. $60,000
    D. $65,000

Question 28

Ross is managing a construction project for the first time. Three months in, he notices that the running cost is higher than expected. So, he decides to assess the project's financial health by calculating the difference between the earned value and the actual cost. What is Ross measuring?

    A. Cost Performance Index
    B. Cost Variance
    C. Planned Value
    D. To-Complete Performance Index

Question 29

A predefined budget allocation is a project _____.

    A. Budget
    B. Assumption
    C. Risk
    D. Constraint

Question 30

Sally is in charge of an ergonomic chair design project. Upon the identification of some technical risks, she decides it's best to create a prototype. This is an example of risk:

    A. Acceptance
    B. Avoidance
    C. Transference
    D. Mitigation

Question 31

Stella works as a project manager at Smart Tools, a company specialized in creating smart kitchen appliances. She has recently completed the design phase of a product and is currently arranging a phase review with the steering committee, which will be facilitated by the company's PMO. Phase reviews are also called:

    A. Kill point
    B. Endpoint
    C. PMO review
    D. Project review

Question 32

Adil is a project manager in charge of creating a next-generation vehicle. Before the assembly of the vehicle can be performed, the wheels have to be designed and built. Which type of dependency does this depict?

A. External

B. Discretionary

C. Soft Logic

D. Mandatory

Question 33

You get assigned by the company management to lead a new project and you're immediately asked to develop the project charter in order to launch the project as soon as possible. To develop the project charter, you will need all of the following documents: (Select three)

A. Strategic plan

B. Business case

C. Agreements

D. Project plan

Question 34

You are the project manager of a construction project. Midway through the execution phase, Mark, a key team member, requests a two-month leave for personal reasons. What should you do first before replying to Mark's leave request?

A. Find a replacement

B. Evaluate the impact of Mark's leave on the project

C. Persuade Mark to take shorter leaves over the remaining project duration instead

D. Ask Mark to postpone his leave

Question 35

Farah uses a predictive approach to manage projects. Despite the $75,000 increase in project costs, she was able to finish the project six weeks ahead of schedule. This situation represents:

A. Resource leveling
B. Resource smoothing
C. Crashing
D. Fast-tracking

Question 36

You are managing a software development project worth $100,000. Referring to the project status report, you find out that you have spent $30,000, with 25% of the work completed. The project is:

A. Under budget
B. Over budget
C. Ahead of schedule
D. Behind schedule

Question 37

Benjamin is a procurement manager assigned to a construction project. He meets with the project manager to assess the project primary vendor's final performance, highlighting the many issues that they experienced with the latter, including late delivery and budget overruns. Benjamin spends more time with the project manager to analyze what they could have done differently and what they did well in addressing the vendor issues as they occurred. What activity are Benjamin and the project manager engaged in?

A. Collaborating on an open claim with the vendor
B. Generating a work performance report
C. Confirming the formal acceptance of the vendor's work
D. Capturing lessons learned

Question 38

You are managing a telecommunication project following the predictive lifecycle. While controlling the project execution, you uncover scope creep. You then discover that it was caused by a key project stakeholder who happens to be also your close friend. What should you do?

    A. Nothing, since the scope creep is a result of a prominent stakeholder and a close friend

    B. Reverse the scope changes since you didn't approve them

    C. Take the scope creep to the change control board

    D. Nothing, since the scope creep could have a positive impact on the project

Question 39

Jana is managing a project to build a water distillation machine. After internally verifying that the product properly extracts essential oils, Jana shipped it to the client site. After receiving the machine, the client sent an email to Jana asking whether it meets their requirements or not. What should Jana do next?

    A. Send an engineer to the client's site to double-check the product requirements

    B. Perform the control quality process and use the contingency reserve to fix any unidentified issues

    C. Collaborate with the client to get their signature approving that the product complies with their requirements

    D. Confirm that the product was internally tested and formally close the project

Question 40

Your project is following a predictive work method. Your team discovers that many implemented features differ from the scope outlined in the project charter. As the project manager, what should you refer to in order to deal with this matter?

    A. Refer to WBS

    B. Refer to WBS dictionary

    C. Refer to the requirements traceability matrix

    D. Refer to the project charter

Question 41

Sally is managing a project consisting of four phases. Which of the following meetings should she hold at each phase to ensure stakeholders' continuous commitment?

    A. kickoff meeting
    B. Retrospective meeting
    C. Risk review meeting
    D. Stage gate meeting

Question 42

Prior to a meeting with the sponsor to update them on the project status, Margaret is going through the project status report which shows that the SPI is 0.8, while the CPI is 1.1. Which area should be more concerning to Margaret?

    A. Nothing, the project is performing well
    B. Cost
    C. Schedule
    D. Risk

Question 43

You are planning a cryptocurrency conference. The Ministry of Finance, which is the conference sponsor, limited the number of attendees to forty. One day prior to the event, you got a call from the ministry office informing you that they wanted to add two other subject matter experts to the conference attendees list. Luckily, the conference room has a seating capacity of fifty people. However, you need to rearrange lodging, catering, coffee breaks, gift packages, etc. accordingly. What should you do first?

    A. Issue a change request to address the ministry's request
    B. Accept the ministry's request and increase the number of attendees since the conference didn't start yet
    C. Accept the ministry's request and increase the number of attendees since the request is issued by the sponsor

D. Refuse to increase the number of attendees since the event is only one day away

Question 44

Muhammed calculates the early & late start and finish dates of his project activities. One of the activities has the following representation. What is this activity's float?

A. 16
B. 8
C. 12
D. 24

Question 45

The _____ is a project forecasting tool that gives you the cost estimate of your project if you continue to perform with the same cost performance.
   A. Estimate to Complete (ETC)
   B. Variance at Completion (VAC)
   C. Estimate at Completion (EAC)
   D. Budget at Completion (BAC)

Question 46

You are managing an eCommerce project using a predictive life cycle. Your customer reached out to you asking to add a new feature to allow users to review the products they purchased.

Knowing that this feature may involve some security risks, what should you do next? (Select two)
  A. Inform the customer of the potential risks to convince them to change their mind
  B. Ask the customer to submit a change request
  C. Protect your team from distraction by asking the customer to put off the change until you finish the project
  D. Evaluate the change and its associated risks with your team

Question 47
Jasmine is managing a highway paving project. Four months into the project, she noticed that the performance is deteriorating. What did she examine to make such a realization?
  A. Status Report
  B. Risk Report
  C. Forecasting Report
  D. Trend Report

Question 48
While managing an industrial project, you noticed that two stakeholders were always debating which may negatively impact the project. Which of the following options is used to document and monitor this type of situation?
  A. Dispute log
  B. Problem log
  C. Change log
  D. Issue log

Question 49
Lia is the project manager of a construction project. Before announcing the completion of the project execution, she reviews deliverables and performs a site walkthrough. What exactly is Lia conducting?
  A. An inspection

B. A handing over

C. An audit

D. A scope validation

Question 50

You work for Kitchen Plus Inc. as a project manager. Their most recent project involves the creation of an automatic dicer with industry-exclusive characteristics. Based on the information provided by your team, the current schedule performance index (SPI) is at 1.10, while the cost performance index (CPI) is at 0.80. What could be a good strategy for balancing out the performance of both the schedule and budget?

    A. Crash the schedule by adding additional resources to critical activities

    B. Fast-track the longest activities that fall on the critical path

    C. Level out resource usage to further spread out costs over time

    D. Nothing, since the project is performing as planned

Predictive approach - Answers

Question 1 = A
Explanation: In a network diagram, the critical path is the path with the longest series of tasks. Activities that are not on the critical path have some float (also called slack) that allows some margin for delay without causing the delay or change of the project end date. Free float is the amount of time an activity can be delayed without delaying the early start of the immediate subsequent activity. The critical chain is also the longest path in the network diagram, but unlike the critical path, it takes into consideration resource availability in addition to technical dependencies. (PMBOK 6th edition, page 210).

Question 2 = C
Explanation: Scope creep (also known as "feature creep" or "requirement creep") refers to the uncontrolled expansion of the project's scope. Customer obsession consists of an excessive focus on providing a better customer experience by meeting and even exceeding your client's needs. However, customer obsession shouldn't mean delivering beyond scope since the latter can increase the project schedule and cost, thus decreasing the success rate of the project. The tackled situation is not considered as gold plating since the client is the one who brought up the change request; it was neither the project manager nor team members who added changes without the client's approval, as gold plating implies.

Question 3 = B
Explanation: As soon as it becomes obvious that your project will be delayed, you should notify your client and present them with new alternatives. You should be honest and transparent about delays. The question includes the term "next", so the first thing that you should do before creating a change request or updating the

lesson learned is meeting with stakeholders to inform them about the situation. Under the RESPONSIBILITY section of the PMI's Code of Ethics and Professional Conduct, page 3: When the project manager discovers errors or omissions caused by others, they should communicate them to the appropriate body as soon as they are discovered. Under the HONESTY section from page 6: the project manager should provide accurate information in a timely manner.

Question 4 = B
Explanation: Anna is identifying stakeholders and analyzing their level of influence. Although the project has been active for two months, it is recommended to permanently perform this activity, especially when the project gets into a new phase.

Question 5 = A
Explanation: Since requirements are fixed and deliverables will only be shipped at the end of the project, then Dany is using a predictive approach. The iterative life cycle is also characterized by a single delivery (Agile Practice Guide, page 18), but it has dynamic requirements. Adaptive and incremental life cycles involve frequent small deliveries. In the described scenario, payment installments are not linked to deliverables or iterations; it's just a payment option that has no connection or influence on the project life cycle.

Question 6 = B
Explanation: Earned Value refers to the value of the work accomplished to date. If the project is terminated today, Earned Value will show you the value that the project has produced. In this case, the project's Earned Value (EV) is $40,000 = 40% of the value of total work. The $60,000 represents the actual cost (AC). The planned value is $50,000 (50% of the budget), while the cost variance is -$20,000 (EV - AC).

Question 7 = D

Explanation: Unlike parametric estimating, the analogous estimating technique uses expert judgment by comparing an activity to a similarly completed one on a previous project in order to determine its duration or cost. This means that Alyssa would rely on expert feedback, i.e., completing a similar task in 14 hours.

Question 8 = B

Explanation: The planned work is included within the lowest level of the WBS components, which is known as work packages. Detailed information on work packages, such as descriptions, owners, prerequisites, successors, due dates, etc. is included in the Work Breakdown Structure Dictionary (PMBOK 6th edition, page 162).

Question 9 = B, C

Explanation: Since it has a 7-day float, this activity is not on the critical path. The float of this activity can be calculated by subtracting the early start (day 5) from the late start (day 12) or by subtracting the early finish (day 10) from the late finish (day 17). Since the float of the activity is greater than zero, then it's not on the critical path. Remember that critical path activities have zero float.

Question 10

A. Construction work requires a building permit from the City council: EEF

B. Workers who don't obey safety rules will be penalized: OPA

C. Only authorized personnel are allowed on site: OPA

D. Workers have expertise in infrastructure construction: EEF

Question 11 = A

Explanation: The Management Reserve is a dedicated budget under "management control" used for unidentified risks during risk analysis, aka unknown-unknowns (unknown= unidentified, unknowns=risks). On the other hand, a contingency reserve is used for identified risks with predetermined risk response strategies, aka known-unknowns (known= identified, Unknowns=risks). Additional reserve and buffer reserve are made-up terms.

Question 12 = B, D
Explanation: Project deliverables can be products, services, or any other types of outcome. In a predictive approach, project deliverables should be determined, described, and agreed upon as early as possible in the project, to avoid any costly changes later on. Acceptance criteria should also be described and agreed upon. The change is possible and should follow the change request process.

Question 13 = B
Explanation: Lag Time is when a delay is purposely made between activities. Lead time, on the other hand, is the time saved by starting an activity before its predecessor is completed. Crashing and fast-tracking are two schedule compression techniques.

Question 14 = B, C
Explanation: This is an example of finish-to-finish mandatory dependency. Two tasks may in fact run concurrently in the case of a finish-to-finish dependency. However, the second task can be entirely completed only after the first task is 100% done. Mandatory dependencies are those that are legally or contractually required or inherent in the nature of the work.

Question 15 = A
Explanation: Brody must discuss the impact of the change request on the project cost with the client. He cannot process the change request unless the client agrees with its impact.

Question 16 = A, B

Explanation: Predictive methods focus on thoroughly analyzing and planning the future while taking into account known risks. The scope, time and cost are all determined early in the project life cycle. Predictive teams will often establish a Change Control Board to ensure that only the most valuable changes are considered for implementation.

Question 17 = B
Explanation: Since the project manager didn't assign the project members themselves, then the organization must be functional. In this case, it is best to talk with functional managers and negotiate clear and written assignments with reliable scheduling priorities. It is the responsibility of functional managers to clearly define the resources' calendar and staff assignments. One of your responsibilities as a project manager is to make sure that functional managers are aware of when resources are required through providing resources' calendar and staff assignments. Adjusting or crashing the schedule without tackling the source of the problem is not an appropriate course of action. Besides, crashing the project implies adding more resources, which is beyond the project manager's authority in a functional organization type.

Question 18 = A
Explanation: A Rough Order of Magnitude Estimate (ROM estimate) is an estimation of the needed effort and cost to complete a project. A ROM estimate takes place very early in a project's life cycle; during the project selection and approval period and prior to project initiation in most cases. The order of magnitude during the initiation phase has an accuracy range of -25% to 75% (PMBOK 6th edition, page 241).

Question 19 = C
Explanation: Cost and schedule baselines are used to assess performance in the monitoring and controlling phases.

Question 20 = C
Explanation: Resource leveling is used to optimize resource allocation by adjusting the activities' start and finish dates. This often results in changing the original critical path, as was the case in the described scenario; John is a scarce resource for the project and his availability is constrained, which led to extending the project schedule to manage this limitation. Resource smoothing, on the other hand, is performed to achieve a more consistent resource utilization over a period of time. Resource loading is the total assigned hours of work divided by the number of hours required to complete it. Load balancing is common in computing and it refers to the process of distributing a set of tasks over a number of resources with the aim of speeding up the overall data processing.

Question 21 = D
Explanation: The WBS is a hierarchical decomposition of the total scope of work to create the required deliverables. The planned work is included in the lowest level of the WBS components, which are called work packages. Product breakdown is a product analysis technique (PMBOK 6th edition, page 153). The product roadmap demonstrates the anticipated sequence of deliverables throughout the project duration. Affinity diagrams classify a large number of ideas into groups for analysis and review.

Question 22 = B
Explanation: The schedule performance index (SPI) is a measure of the conformance of actual progress (earned value) to the planned progress: SPI = EV / PV. A value of 1.0 indicates that the project performance is on target. When CPI or SPI is greater than 1.0, it indicates better-than-planned project performance, while a CPI or SPI that is less than 1.0 indicates poorer-than-planned project performance.

EV = 10% x $100,000 = $10,000, PV = (1 Month / 10 Months) x $100, 000 = $10,000 then SPI = EV / PV = 1

Question 23 = D
Explanation: The bottom-up method is a way to estimate an overall value by approximating values for smaller components and using the total sum of these values as the overall value. This type of estimation is used to create the project schedule or budget. The project work is typically subdivided into smaller parts and each component is given a duration and cost estimate. The individual duration estimates are aggregated to determine the schedule, while the individual cost estimates are aggregated to determine the budget.

Question 24 = B
Explanation: Risk acceptance acknowledges the existence of a threat, but no proactive action is taken. The most common active acceptance strategy is to establish a contingency reserve, including time, money, or resources to handle the threat if it occurs. Passive acceptance involves no proactive action apart from a periodic review of the threat to ensure that it does not change significantly (PMBOK 6th edition, page 443). A workaround is an unplanned response to deal with unidentified risks and risks that are passively accepted.

Question 25 = A
Explanation: Resource calendar is a calendar for planning, managing, and monitoring resources, including both employees and equipment. It gives project managers an overview of how resources are being utilized, which resources are available, and when. On the other hand, the Responsibility Assignment Matrix (RAM) describes the involvement of different parties and their roles in completing tasks or deliverables in a project. It's used to clarify roles and responsibilities within a team, project, or process. RACI is an acronym for Responsible Accountable Consult and Inform and it's

used to assign roles and responsibilities for each task in a given process. An organigram, also called an organizational chart, organogram, or organizational breakdown structure (OBS), is a diagram that depicts the organization's structure and the relationships and ranks of its different positions.

Question 26 = C
Explanation: A resource breakdown structure is a hierarchical list of team and physical resources related by category and resource type that is used for project planning, management, and control. Each descending level corresponds to a more detailed description of the resource. A resource calendar, on the other hand, is a calendar for planning, managing, and monitoring resources. Organizational Breakdown Structure (OBS), also known as Organization Chart, is used for representing the project organization. RACI is an acronym for Responsible Accountable Consult and Inform and it's used to assign the roles and responsibilities of the individuals involved in a project or a process.

Question 27 = D
Explanation: The total cost of the contract is the sum of the Actual cost and the Fixed fee; $60,000 + $5,000 = $65,000.

Question 28 = B
Explanation: The amount of budget deficit or surplus at a given point in time, expressed as the difference between earned value and the actual cost, is known as Cost Variance (PMBOK 6th edition, page 262).

Question 29 = D
Explanation: Project constraints are limiting factors for your project that can impact delivery, quality, and overall project success. An imposed delivery date or a predefined budget are considered project constraints.

Question 30 = D
Explanation: Mitigation may involve prototype development to reduce the risk of scaling up. Generating a prototype will support the testing and from this testing, you can generate the data necessary to probably close out a risk item. To keep costs low, you may opt for partial prototypes for the specific portions of the process where the risk is concentrated.

Question 31 = A
Explanation: Phase reviews, aka phase gates, phase exits, phase entrances, kill points, and stage gates, is a formal review of the project to evaluate its status. The results are documented and presented to the concerned stakeholders or the sponsor in order to get their approval to proceed to the next phase in the project lifecycle. It's called "Kill point" because when your board determines that your project hasn't achieved its objectives to date, they may decide to stop it.

Question 32 = D
Explanation: A mandatory dependency is also called a hard dependency or hard logic. For example, consider 2 activities A and B, if B has a mandatory dependency on A, it means action on B cannot be performed until action on A has been completed. A discretionary or soft logic dependency, on the other hand, is an optional or preferred dependency. External dependencies involve a relationship between project activities and non-project activities (PMBOK 6th edition, pages 191-192).

Question 33 = A, B, C
Explanation: To develop the Project Charter, the project manager needs the business documents such as the business case, benefits/strategic plan, and agreements. The project plan is developed once the project charter is signed.

Question 34 = B
Explanation: The first thing you should do in this situation is to understand what impact this leave will have on the project. For instance, a two-month leave for a 3-year project may not have a big impact, but it will have a significant impact on a 6-month project if the team member is a key player. After evaluating the impact, you can ask Mark to postpone his leave or split it into shorter leaves over the project life cycle. If the impact of Mark's leave is still significant, then you may need to seek a replacement.

Question 35 = C
Explanation: Project crashing occurs when you reduce the time of one or more tasks in order to minimize the overall duration of a project. Crashing is done by increasing the project resources, which helps make tasks take less time than planned. However, this leads to a rise in project costs. Such measures cannot be implemented without the approval of the sponsor or key stakeholders. Fast-tracking is also a schedule compression technique, but it involves performing tasks simultaneously without adding more resources or increasing costs. Resource leveling and resource smoothing are two resource optimization techniques, which are used to respond to resource limitations. These two techniques can only extend the project schedule.

Question 36 = B
Explanation: You can determine the financial status of the project by calculating the Cost Performance Index (CPI = EV / AC) or the Cost Variance (CV = EV - AC). Since AC = $30,000, then you need to calculate the Earned Value (EV = % completed work x budget). Considering the described scenario, EV= 25% x $100,000 = $25,000.
Consequently, CPI = $25,000 / $30,000 = 0.833 which is less than 1, so your project is over budget. CV = $25,000 - $30,000 = -

$5,000 which is less than 0, which confirms that the project is over budget.

Question 37 = D
Explanation: Benjamin and the project manager are discussing lessons learned in engaging with this particular vendor and also in activities associated with managing the vendor's performance. This includes identifying what went well and what could have been done differently, which will benefit future projects.

Question 38 = C
Explanation: The scope creep should be brought to the project team's attention and treated as an unapproved change. This will also need to go through the formal channel by reporting it to the change control board and decide with them on the appropriate course of action (PMBOK 6th edition, page 115). Undoing the changes without referring to the CCB means you are going to perform additional work that is not part of the scope, resulting in further scope creep: That's why you need approval from CCB. As a project manager, you should avoid favoritism and conflict-of-interest situations by maintaining impartiality in your decisions.

Question 39 = C
Explanation: At this stage, Jana should work with the client to get their signature approving that the product complies with requirements. Confirming that the product has been internally tested on your part is not sufficient since the client must validate that the product does meet their requirements. The control quality process is supposed to be performed before the product is shipped. In this situation, the client just asked whether the product met requirements or not and didn't report any problems. Thus, the proper next step is to go over all of the product specifications with the client to formally validate them and get their signature

approving that the product complies with requirements in order to finally close the project.

Question 40 = C
Explanation: Traceability Matrix is a document that maps requirements as well as other aspects of a project. It's used as evidence to confirm that requirements have been fulfilled, as it typically documents those requirements along with issues and test results.

Question 41 = D
Explanation: Stage-gate or phase review meetings represent an opportunity for project stakeholders to review project progress along with planned future actions. In these meetings, project stakeholders can assess whether or not the project is on track to meet the organization's expectations. You should schedule gate meetings at key milestones throughout your project to not only ensure it is on track but also demonstrate to the project stakeholders that you are staying on course.

Question 42 = C
Explanation: Since the Schedule Performance Index (SPI) is less than 1.0, then the project is behind schedule. Consequently, Margret should be concerned about the project schedule. Since CPI is 1.1, then the project is under budget. Thus, Margaret's project is on track cost-wise. There is no indication in the question that Margaret should be concerned about risks.

Question 43 = A
Explanation: When a critical key stakeholder requests a change you should consider their request with high priority and issue a change request to the Change Control Board (CCB) in order to add their request to the scope. In the described situation, the project manager is able to address the stakeholder request. So, it's not

appropriate to decline the change request under the pretext that the conference date is only one day away. On the other hand, you should not immediately increase the number of attendees because this will be considered as scope creep. Even though the conference hasn't yet started, project execution has already begun since the project team has contacted suppliers, reserved attendees' accommodations, booked the conference room, etc.

Question 44 = B
Explanation: Float, Total float, Slack, or activity float represent how long an activity can be delayed without causing the delay of the project completion date. On a critical path, the total float is zero. You can calculate an activity float by subtracting the Early Start date of the activity from its Late Start date: (12 - 4 = 8 days), or by subtracting the Early Finish date of the activity from its Late Finish date (28 - 20 = 8 days).

Question 45 = C
Explanation: Estimate at Completion (EAC) is defined as the sum of the completed work cost plus the cost required to finish the remaining work. Estimate at Completion (EAC) may differ from the Budget At Completion (BAC) based on the project performance. If it becomes obvious that the BAC is no longer viable, the project manager should consider the forecasted EAC instead.

Question 46 = B, D
Explanation: Since you are working under a predictive life cycle, you should ask the customer to submit a change request for you and your team to evaluate. The change request evaluation should cover analyzing its associated risks and implications. After gathering all information, the Change Control Board (CCB) will decide to either accept the change or reject it. The project manager is usually a member of the CCB. In this case, you may influence the decision based on the conducted analysis. But, you cannot do this

without assessing the change with your team first. The customer may not accept to postpone the change. The concept of protecting the team from distraction or external interference doesn't exist in the predictive approach; it's rather common in the Scrum framework, more specifically during sprint execution.

Question 47 = D
Explanation: A trend Report is used to check the performance status; whether it's on track, improving, or deteriorating over a time period. This report shows a comparison between the project's current performance in a specific duration against its previous performance during a similar time duration (comparing monthly performances for example). Performance could be compared monthly, quarterly, semesterly, or annually.

Question 48 = D
Explanation: The issue log, also called an issue register, is a project document that records and tracks all issues that have a negative impact on the project. Once created, it'll be your tool to monitor and communicate all that is going on in the project. Such issues may involve resources leaving the project, conflicting teams, or even individuals with low morale. Change log is used to record all change requests. Problem log and dispute log are both made-up terms.

Question 49 = A
Explanation: During an inspection, the project manager reviews deliverables and performs a site walkthrough if applicable. Audits, on the other hand, are carried out to determine if project activities comply with organizational and project policies, processes, and procedures (PMBOK 6th edition, page 294). In other words, audits are performed on processes while inspections are performed on products. Lia is neither validating the scope with the customer nor handing over deliverables to them.

Question 50 = C

Explanation: Based on the performance indexes provided, while the project is 10% ahead of schedule, it is over budget. Leveling out resource usage is a strategy used to spread out costs over time. This helps to reduce unexpected spikes in spending, albeit it may lead to lengthening the schedule. Crashing or fast-tracking are two schedule compression techniques. So, it's pointless to use them in the described situation since the project is ahead of schedule.

Full mock exam

Question 1
Joining a new company as a project manager, Mia is facing some struggles; her superiors noticed that during a kick-off meeting, she had difficulty responding to questions about how the project fits in with the organization's objectives. What critical skill is Mia lacking?
   A. Business management and strategic skills
   B. Technical project management skills
   C. Communication skills
   D. Leadership skills

Question 2
Violet got signed up to manage an eco-friendly packaging project. In order to manage involved stakeholders, she first analyzes their power, urgency, and legitimacy. Which analysis method is Violet applying?
   A. Stakeholder cube
   B. Salience model
   C. Power/interest grid
   D. Power/influence grid

Question 3
Oliver notices that his colleague Darnell, who is a fellow project manager, shows up at the office with new high-tech gadgets every day. This raises his suspicions that Darnell might be accepting gifts from hardware vendors who will bid on one of your company's upcoming multimillion-dollar contracts. Which of the following should Oliver do?
   A. Tell Darnell that such gifts aren't appropriate and leave it at that
   B. Convince Darnell to return the items and stop accepting any gifts from vendors

C. Ask Darnell directly whether these items were gifts from vendors or he purchased them himself

D. Report Darnell to the organization so that a conflict-of-interest investigation can take place

Question 4

Zoe is a project manager working on a contract. As the project comes to closure, and she completes her contract, she finds herself out of work. What type of organizational structure does Zoe work in?

A. Strong matrix

B. Projectized organization

C. Functional organization

D. Weak matrix

Question 5

Ethan is the CEO of Men In, a Men luxury lifestyle gadgets company. After deciding to invest even more in the project management capabilities of the organization, he established a PMO that will ensure compliance with a set of project management standards. What type of PMO is Ethan implementing?

A. Supportive

B. Controlling

C. Directive

D. Agile

Question 6

You get hired to lead the marketing department of a financial institution. You first meet with your project management team in order to review the project portfolio. Next, you focus on learning about the governance framework in place, which is considered to be:

A. Organizational process assets

B. Project management framework

C. Enterprise environmental factors

D. Agile Manifesto principles

Question 7

You are a lead project manager for a construction company, which has recently gone through major organizational changes. Rebecca, the new manager, seems to be closely monitoring when employees arrive and leave work. You overhear her saying that she is concerned about the team's lack of motivation. What type of management style does Rebecca exhibit?

A. Theory X

B. Theory Y

C. Theory Z

D. Theory XY

Question 8

Ali is a risk manager working in collaboration with the project manager to perform a risk analysis. To determine the most likely project completion date based on known risks, they conduct a simulation using the _____tool that will go through thousands of possible scenarios.

A. Monte Carlo analysis

B. Decision-tree analysis

C. Sensitivity analysis

D. Influence diagrams

Question 9

William is a project manager who follows the servant leader approach. He is currently onboarding a new team member who he believes can help fill skill-level gaps in his current project team. William provides the new team member with a copy of the project charter and commits to sending him a copy of _____, which addresses team values, ground rules, and working agreements.

A. The employment contract
B. The resource management plan
C. The communication management plan
D. The team charter

Question 10
The project you are managing has become so large (multiple teams, long duration, and huge budget) that the single sponsor has been replaced by a steering committee. What should you do to accommodate this new change?
A. Acknowledge that the stakeholders' structure has changed and tailor communication accordingly
B. Work according to the original plan while keeping in mind that the project may now include additional stakeholders
C. Hold a meeting with the new steering committee and continue working on the project
D. Share an updated status report with the new committee

Question 11
Your company must select one of two projects that have the same budget, but different levels of risks and returns. Which tool or technique should you use to help your company make the right decision?
A. Decision tree
B. Tornado diagram
C. SWOT Analysis
D. Sensitivity analysis

Question 12
Lucas is a government contractor. In the new project he is working on, he wants to keep costs under control while putting the risk on the vendor's side. Moreover, Lucas wants to ensure that the seller is legally obliged to complete the contract, otherwise, they may face

financial liabilities. Which type of contract best conforms to Lucas' needs and represents the least risk for him as a buyer?

A. Fixed-price

B. Time and materials (T&M)

C. Cost-plus incentive fee

D. Cost-reimbursement

Question 13

You are leading a small team of developers using project management software with a Kanban board. As you always receive questions from your team members on how to create, review, and validate tasks or issues, you decide to create the following chart. This chart is called:

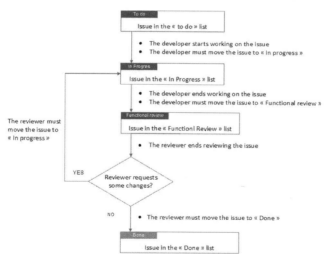

A. Pareto chart

B. Flowchart

C. Context diagram

D. Scatter diagram

Question 14

Eliza is the project manager of a 3D home design project. After setting the time of daily standup meetings, she faced some issues since not all of her remote team members agreed on the set time. Which conflict resolution technique should Eliza use to handle time zone differences?

A. Avoid

B. Accommodate

C. Compromise

D. Withdrawal

Question 15

While conducting remote resource hiring, what is the best way to quickly collect data from resources to analyze and compare?

A. Video recordings

B. Workshops

C. Questionnaires and surveys

D. Live interviews

Question 16

Tom is a project manager at Tunitalent, an innovative design, web, and marketing agency. He suggested to his manager to create a dropshipping e-commerce project since he had heard that it's a trendy and profitable project. Tom's manager refuses since Tunitalent lacks experience in this field. Being excited to go through such a new experience and confident in his ability to successfully manage the project, what should Tom do to persuade his manager to select the project?

A. Conduct a what-if analysis

B. Calculate the Return On Investment (ROI)

C. Calculate the Net Present Value (NPV)

D. Conduct a cost-benefit analysis of the business case

Question 17

Rachel is running a project with remote and local resources. Her remote team complains that they are not getting enough information about what's going on with the project, which has caused them to do some rework. Rachel scheduled a conference call with the two teams, and they decided to switch to a sophisticated enterprise chat platform to optimize communication. What conflict resolution technique is Rachel using?

A. Collaborate
B. Compromise
C. Force
D. Smooth

Question 18

To better understand how the project's system flows, depicting the scope in abstraction, and enabling stakeholders to communicate about it, and what lies beyond its boundaries, you use a visual representation of how people and other systems interact with a new system. Which of the following tools do you use?

A. Affinity Diagram
B. Flowchart
C. Context diagram
D. Influence diagram

Question 19

Realizing that his project is not going according to estimations, Robert suspects that it might be due to Student Syndrome. What does it mean?

A. People who proceed with their studies during their professional careers but are unable to balance both
B. People who begin to apply themselves only at the last possible moment before the deadline

C. People who experience a learning curve whenever they are working on a project

D. Professional project managers who consider themselves continuous learners

Question 20

You are managing a project using the Scrum framework. You receive a call from the product owner asking for a meeting with the team to discuss the possible approaches to implement user stories and make some initial size estimations. What type of meeting is the product owner referring to?

A. Sprint planning

B. Story mapping

C. Backlog refinement

D. Brainstorming

Question 21

Constraints and assumptions are important for your project. They need to be identified, controlled, and monitored continuously. Wrong assumptions or constraints can impact your project. For instance, when a constraint turns out to be false, it affects your project:

A. Positively

B. Negatively

C. Depends on the constraint

D. Depends on the project

Question 22

Three assembly lines are producing 5 mm diameter cylindrical steel bars. You perform a quality inspection by taking 10 random bars from each line. The following are the inspection results in mm measurements. Line 1 results can be described as:

	Bar 1	Bar 2	Bar 3	Bar 4	Bar 5	Bar 6	Bar 7	Bar 8	Bar 9	Bar 10
Line 1	4.45	4.50	4.40	4.45	4.40	4.45	4.50	4.45	4.40	4.45
Line 2	5.10	5.15	4.90	4.90	4.85	4.95	5.05	5.00	5.00	5.10
Line 3	5.00	5.05	4.95	4.95	5.05	5.00	5.05	5.00	5.05	5.10

A. Accurate
B. Precise
C. Both accurate and precise
D. Neither accurate nor precise

Question 23

The organization that Wyatt is working for has a matrix structure. Since the organization is big, the communication channels are complex and cross-functional. Wyatt occasionally communicates with his coworkers in other departments along with several team members working under him. He also reports back to his boss. What type of communication is this?

A. Horizontal communication
B. Vertical communication
C. Parallel communication
D. Triangular communication

Question 24

Taariq is having trouble getting one of his team members to complete their assigned tasks. He invites him over to watch a football game. After the game, Taariq talks with the team member about his performance issues. What type of communication is this?

A. Para-lingual
B. Visual
C. Formal verbal
D. Informal verbal

Question 25

You are the project manager of a rebranding project. When the execution was completed, several key stakeholders, including the sponsor, were reluctant to accept deliverables and close the project. What should you do in this situation? (Select three)

    A. Identify and resolve any open issues. Then, be firm on formal closure.

    B. Formally close the project. Stakeholders will get well-acquainted with the new brand by that time.

    C. Identify and openly discuss the reasons for reluctance.

    D. Invite earnest feedback from all sides and try to identify any misunderstanding.

Question 26

Lauren believes that being an active listener is not easy. She considers active listening to be more of an art than a skill, so she often encourages her team members to use a checklist including all key elements of active listening before any important meeting with stakeholders. Which of the following are regarded as elements of active listening? (Select three)

    A. Making eye contact

    B. Paraphrasing

    C. Interpreting the information

    D. Interrupting when appropriate

Question 27

The final decision on which projects are selected for execution generally falls to the executives of the company. However, Miriam was always able to use her experience as a project manager to assist her organization's decision-makers in choosing the ideal project through the use of the suitable benefit measurement project selection method. Which of the following is not a benefit measurement project selection method?

    A. 5 whys

    B. Internal Rate of Return

C. Scoring model

D. Discounted cash flow

Question 28

Sabrina is a project manager for Steel Foundations. She has been brought on to the project in the very early stages and has been asked to write the charter for it. Over the past week, she met with a number of stakeholders, received their input, and is now ready to have the charter signed. Who is normally responsible for signing the project charter?

A. Project Sponsor

B. Senior Management

C. Project Manager

D. Project stakeholders

Question 29

As a project manager, your authority and power vary depending on whether you work in a functional, matrix, or projectized organization. Once appointed as a project manager, inherent forms of legitimate power will be conveyed to you. There are three forms of legitimate power:

A. Absolute, direct, and indirect

B. Formal, informal, and persuasive

C. Formal, reward, and direct

D. Formal, reward, and penalty

Question 30

You are managing a small project with a total of 4 stakeholders. You have recently added a new team member. What is the current number of communication channels?

A. 4

B. 5

C. 10

D. 20

Question 31

When discussing your choice to opt for remote resources with the project sponsor, you enumerated the many advantages of working with remote teams. You mentioned all of the following advantages, except:

A. Access to more skilled resources
B. Less travel and relocation expenses
C. Utilization of a war room
D. Reduction of time spent commuting

Question 32

Stan is managing a project using the predictive approach. After identifying a risk, he decides to transfer it to another party through:

A. Buying insurance
B. Accepting a lower profit if some activities overrun
C. Asking the sponsor to deal with the risk
D. Eliminating risk through beta testing

Question 33

What characterizes Carter's management style is that he gives freedom to his team members to make decisions, expecting them to solve issues on their own. Allowing teams to make their own decisions and set their own objectives is referred to as:

A. Transactional leadership
B. Servant leadership
C. Laissez-faire leadership
D. Interactional leadership

Question 34

All of the following statements are true, except:

A. A project can have several stakeholders
B. A program is a big project
C. Portfolio management is aligned with organizational strategy

D. Multiple projects can be aligned with one program

Question 35

You came across one of your software project's key stakeholders in the company hallway. You seized the opportunity to get their feedback. They were impressed with the project progress, requesting that you urgently add a new user story for marketing the product. How should you respond to this request?

A. Welcome their request and add the user story to the sprint backlog

B. Add the user story to the product backlog and schedule it for the next sprint to protect the team from disruptions

C. Add the user story to the product backlog and let the product owner decide its priority

D. Refuse to create the user story since it's the product owner's responsibility to maintain and refine the product backlog

Question 36

The amount of time a task can be postponed without affecting the subsequent tasks or the overall completion of the project is referred to as: (Select two)

A. Buffer

B. Float

C. Independent activity

D. Slack

Question 37

This is Ela's first time managing an agile project. Knowing that she opted for Scrum as a framework, which of the following options describes her new team?

A. The team ranges in size from three to nine members

B. All of her team members must have a technical background

C. Team members are all I-shaped

D. Team members are dependent on the scrum master

Question 38

As a senior business analyst, Brighton was designated to head his organization's project selection committee. After shortlisting a number of potential projects, the selection committee will make its decision based on each project's benefit to cost ratio. Which of the following projects should the committee select?

A. Project A which has a BCR of 6:3
B. Project B which has a BCR of 6:2
C. Project C which has a BCR of 8:2
D. Project D which has a BCR of 3:1

Question 39

You are the manager of a web application project using the Agile approach. During the first sprint, your team completed 4 tasks with story points 3, 5, 8, and 2 respectively. They also finished half of a 13-story-points-worth task. What is the velocity of your team?

A. 18
B. 24.5
C. 31
D. 13

Question 40

Facing a quality issue, you decide to use the _____, a basic tool of quality management that uses the 80/20 Rule to identify top priority defects.

A. Fishbone Diagram
B. Pareto Chart
C. PERT Chart
D. Flowchart

Question 41

Kevin is submitting a number of potential projects to management for selection and approval. Since the organization is currently facing financial challenges, Kevin has been told that it cannot invest more than $350,000 per project, with a leeway of 5% on either side. The 5% leeway is part of:

A. Organizational process assets
B. Enterprise environmental factors
C. Threats
D. Risks

Question 42

Doren, a product owner, started her day with a sprint planning meeting to discuss and set the upcoming sprint goal and backlog. Which of the following options is correct regarding the sprint planning meeting?

A. A discussion between the product owner, the scrum master, and the cross-functional team
B. A discussion between the cross-functional team members only
C. A discussion between the product owner and the scrum master
D. A discussion between the scrum master and the cross-functional team members

Question 43

David is leading a hotel construction project in a foreign country where corruption is widely spread. Since he is having trouble obtaining the required construction permits from local authorities, a member of David's team suggested that he give a bribe to the local officials to get things going and execute the project without issues. How should David react?

A. He should not give the bribe
B. He should give the bribe
C. He should negotiate a non-monetary bribe
D. He should discuss the matter with his superior

Question 44

Moana was assigned for a park redevelopment project where the area will be cleaned and equipped for local families and residents. Since the project has multiple phases and different types of tasks to execute, it involves many stakeholders. How should Moana manage this large number of stakeholders?

A. Ignore low-power stakeholders
B. Only manage the dominating stakeholders
C. Find a way to manage all stakeholders
D. Only manage high power and high-interest stakeholders

Question 45

Wagner is a product owner for a high-quality clothing project. He joins the project team and other prominent stakeholders for a meeting to review a demonstration of the produced deliverable. Wagner attends this type of meeting _____ since the project employs an iteration-based Agile approach.

A. At the beginning of every iteration
B. At the end of every iteration
C. At the end of the project
D. At the start of the project

Question 46

Fabrice is an organization operating in the Oil and Gas industry. They had signed a subcontracting agreement with SPM Inc. to get provided with experts, technical know-how, and mechanical spare parts. Since Fabrice's projects consist in building innovative high-tech machines, the exact description of the work involved is not clear. In this scenario, what kind of contract should they sign with SPM Inc.?

A. Fixed Price Incentive Fee (FPIF)
B. Cost Plus Award Fee (CPAF)
C. Time and Materials (T&M)
D. Firm-Fixed-Price (FFP)

Question 47

Lamont was assigned by his superiors to lead a big project. Since this project is really important for his organization, management does not want any delay in completion. Once he got the project charter signed, Lamont started identifying and categorizing stakeholders using various data representation tools. Which of the following tools can he use? (Select three)

A. Brainwriting
B. Stakeholder cube
C. Direction of influence
D. Salience model

Question 48

Tim, an ambitious project manager, has decided to get PMP certified in a two-month period. He has created an exam preparation plan in which he'll study for 4 weeks, take mock practice tests in weeks 5 and 6, and then take the 7th week off before sitting for the exam in week 8. At the end of week 5, Tim was caught in an accident that kept him hospitalized for one week. To make up for the lost time, he had to move his week off (week 7) up to week 5, and work on mock tests in weeks 6 and 7 instead of weeks 5 and 6. This is an example of:

A. Adaptability
B. Risk mitigation
C. Workaround
D. Corrective action

Question 49

In agile, what is the planning poker technique used for?

A. Estimating how much effort is needed for completing tasks
B. Estimating how much work is left for the sprint
C. Testing the project and identifying blockers
D. Measuring the sprint velocity

Question 50

Hailey is simultaneously managing six projects in her company. Two projects are of a similar type, while the other four are entirely different. Hailey is a _____ in the organization.

A. Portfolio manager
B. Program manager
C. Project manager
D. Program coordinator

Question 51

During the iteration review, the project team was demonstrating new features to the Product Owner. The latter was resting their hands on the table with a relaxed and open posture, occasionally fiddling with their pen or coffee mug without looking directly at the speaker. What kind of communication is the product owner showing? (Select two)

A. Paralingual communication
B. Active listening
C. Implicit message
D. Non-verbal communication

Question 52

While traditional project management functions mainly by following strict phases, sticking to the original requirements and design plan established at the start of the project, Agile project development processes typically:

A. Encapsulate analysis, design, implementation, and test within an iteration
B. Document, estimate, and sequence each planned activity in detail
C. Use a Gantt chart with well-defined activities, responsibilities, and time frames
D. Map the iteration backlog to a Work Breakdown Structure (WBS)

Question 53

The burn-up and burn-down charts are tools used by Scrum teams to get insights into a sprint's work development. Both charts are primarily used for:

A. Identifying technical issues
B. Tracking project progress
C. Project retrospective
D. Sprint planning

Question 54

Barbara is managing an internal design project. She needs a driller with a rental cost of $25 per day, which she finds quite high. Since she will be using it for a long duration, a team member suggests that they can buy this driller for $500. What is the minimum number of rental days before it becomes more advantageous to buy the driller?

A. 2
B. 5
C. 10
D. 20

Question 55

Laila is assigned to lead a new project that requires a hybrid method. Therefore, she enrolled in a course to learn how to tailor her project management approach by combining agile principles with predictive techniques. Which aspect of the PMI talent triangle is Laila developing here?

A. Strategic and Business Management
B. Leadership
C. Technical Project Management
D. Functional Project Management

Question 56

In order to predict your project's future performance based on its current performance, you can use all of the following methods for forecasting purposes: (Select three)

A. Scenario building
B. Simulation
C. Time series method
D. Variance analysis

Question 57

Your organization is conducting several projects, each with its own due date. The available resources must be simultaneously assigned to different projects. Fearing that your project might face some delays, you meet with the functional manager to discuss additional resource allocation to your project. Which of the following is probably the most important skill that you will need for that?

A. Planning
B. Negotiating
C. Facilitating
D. Documenting

Question 58

As an experienced project manager, Nadine believes that managers should embrace transparency in their projects, as its many benefits often outweigh its disadvantages. However, she thinks that, while it is favorable to share many aspects with your team, there are a few things that shouldn't be shared with everyone. As a project manager, Nadine must be transparent about:

A. Confidential information
B. Proprietary information
C. Unproven information and gossip
D. Her decision-making processes

Question 59

Your manufacturing company is adopting lean principles. A quarterly internal audit is performed to verify whether projects are adhering to these principles. In the last audit, auditors noticed that you are delivering as fast as possible, but deciding as late as possible. Based on this statement, is your company complying with lean principles?

A. No, you should both deliver and decide as late as possible
B. No, you should both deliver and decide as fast as possible
C. No, you should deliver as late as possible but decide as fast as possible
D. Yes, it does.

Question 60

Omar is the project manager of a multinational project, in which team members have different cultural backgrounds and nationalities. Despite the fact that all members speak English fluently, what should Omar bear in mind?

A. Since there are cultural differences, he should create a separate code of conduct for each nationality.
B. He may have to just accept that some team members may face some difficulties when working with colleagues of other nationalities.
C. Spoken communications can cause misunderstandings that may not occur in written communications. Such misunderstandings are also hard to identify.
D. Certain groups won't mind late-night meetings and video conferences.

Question 61

Josh is managing an industrial project. He needs a lot of 1000 identical filters which will be custom-made for the project. Due to their high importance, Josh chose a reliable and well-known supplier for producing the filters. Knowing that a tested filter should be thrown away since it couldn't be reutilized, what should Josh do?

A. Conduct a 0% inspection since he trusts that his supplier will deliver the filters according to his specifications.

B. Order more than 1000 filters to perform acceptance sampling on the batch surplus.

C. Require the seller to provide a conformance certificate of the filter's raw materials.

D. Conduct a 100% inspection upon delivery, then order another batch of 1000 filters if satisfied with the quality.

Question 62

During project execution, Nadine found out that tasks were not being performed in the right order at the right time, which resulted in rework and bad morale among the project team. Which project management tool should Nadine implement to deal with this type of issue?

A. Organization chart

B. RACI matrix

C. Communications management plan

D. Work authorization system

Question 63

Mario has taken over the management of a climate-smart agriculture project, replacing the project manager who quitted. The project is at the beginning of its execution phase when Mario notices that his team members have different opinions concerning project work and deliverables, as well as the overall complexity level. What should Mario do right away?

A. He should not intervene. Instead, he should allow his team enough time to get familiar with the project scope

B. He should identify and assess potential risks caused by this divergence of opinion, then develop a plan to manage and respond to these risks

C. He should organize a meeting involving all team members to identify and resolve misunderstandings in order to avoid issues, disintegration, and rework.

D. He should talk to each team member separately to explain the project requirements

Question 64

Katlyn, a project manager at Max Data, has just put the finishing touches on her final project report before meeting with her manager. She spent the last few weeks trying to get the lessons learned feedback from project participants for the final report. For what reasons did Katlyn organize lessons learned? (Select three)

A. Lessons learned databases are an important element of the organizational process assets

B. Lessons learned should focus on identifying individuals accountable for failures and errors

C. Lessons learned meetings should include recommendations for future performance improvements

D. Phase-end lessons learned workshops should represent a good team-building exercise for project members

Question 65

After a long wait, you get a phone call from your project sponsor confirming that the budget has been allocated and the project can get started. They also inform you that the project life cycle should be defined as soon as possible while the kick-off meeting can be scheduled within the next two weeks. You replied by saying that you must first receive the project charter. What is the purpose of a project charter?

A. To document the project life cycle

B. To formally authorize a project and document its initial requirements

C. To use it as a reference during the project kick-off meeting

D. To set up the project code of conduct

Question 66

Chang is the project manager of MCN electric motorcycles. As part of the project quality control process, he decided to check only 10% of the manufactured motorbikes for environmental control. Which technique is Chang using?

A. Sample Selection
B. Control Charts
C. Statistical Sampling
D. Pareto Diagram

Question 67

A local school is planning to use a screening system to select vegetables and fruits suppliers for their "Healthy minds" organic meals project. Which of the following is an example of a screening system?

A. You interview all the vendors and make your decision based on the interviews
B. You negotiate with all the vendors and engage the one who offers the best price
C. You only consider vendors with more than $10,000 revenue in the last financial year
D. You engage the vendor who responds first to your announcement

Question 68

The project's business analyst, Darla, is performing Earned Value Reporting. The project's CPI is 0.9 and the budget at completion is $900. What is the estimated cost at completion?

A. $819
B. $810
C. $900
D. $1,000

Question 69
Depending on who is using them, bids, tenders, and quotes can take on different meanings. But, initially, they can be used interchangeably with:
  A. Proposals
  B. Make-or-buy decisions
  C. Buyer responses
  D. Pre-bid conferences

Question 70
The Agile triangle of constraints is different from the traditional triangle because it allows:
  A. Cost to vary while scope and time are fixed
  B. Cost and time to vary while the scope is fixed
  C. Scope and time to vary while the cost is fixed
  D. Scope to vary while cost and time are fixed

Question 71
Maria is evaluating a potential industrial project. To determine whether its anticipated financial gains will outweigh its present-day investment, she is using the Net Present Value (NPV) as an effective tool to help her determine whether the project will be profitable or not. For instance, NPV > 0 means:
  A. The project will lose money
  B. The project will break even
  C. The project is profitable
  D. We can't know until the ROI is calculated

Question 72
In an effort to increase your agile knowledge, you have been paired with Agile project managers to observe how they lead their teams. You notice that many project decisions are the responsibility of the project team, while project managers are more facilitative than authoritative by sharing a common vision and allowing the team to

focus on their work. What leadership approach have these project managers adopted?

A. Participative leadership
B. Autocratic leadership
C. Transformational leadership
D. Servant leadership

Question 73

Lauren manages a project with a highly talented team. Her team members have diverse skills and expertise that she wants to encourage them to pool their knowledge on project issues in order to make optimal decisions. Which management style is the most appropriate for Lauren to use?

A. Laissez-faire
B. Democratic
C. Autocratic
D. Directive

Question 74

Over the last couple of years, your organization has grown into a corporate group by taking over a number of companies in the same field. This significantly increased the number of its projects, programs, and portfolios. How many active portfolios should be managed concurrently by an organization?

A. One portfolio at a time
B. Based on the size of resources allocated to portfolio management
C. Each portfolio manager should handle only one at a time
D. As many as the organization can handle

Question 75

Dina is a project manager at Clinica Labs, a biopharmaceutical corporation. She intends to talk to her manager about obtaining additional resources for complex activities that her team is unable to perform. These resources will roll off the project as soon as the activities are completed. Which of the following skills does Dina require the most in this situation?

A. Planning skills to identify resource requirements
B. Interpersonal skills to convince her manager
C. Interviewing skills to hire the required resources
D. Technical skills to respond to the risk associated with adding more resources

Question 76

Tom reported to his manager that he had successfully passed his PMP certification exam. Some of his colleagues are aware that this is inaccurate since they also took the exam with Tom and he happened to share the results with them. What are they supposed to do in this situation?

A. Give Tom an opportunity to set things right otherwise report him to PMI
B. Hide the truth since Tom is their friend and colleague and they should support him no matter what
C. Confront Tom and give him a hard time to teach him a lesson
D. Immediately inform their manager and report the violation to PMI directly

Question 77

The knowledge that is garnered from personal experience is the type of information that would be the most difficult to express, articulate, or write down. This type of knowledge is known as:

A. Explicit knowledge
B. Tacit knowledge
C. Tangible knowledge
D. Formal knowledge

Question 78

Mason has just joined a new organization. Wanting to ensure his efficiency as a new project manager, what should Mason's primary focus be?

A. Showcase his project management knowledge

B. Choose a skillful team

C. Assess the organization's culture

D. Get to know the executive managers

Question 79

A project manager is facilitating a meeting to define user stories for the upcoming iteration. Two of their team members, Charlotte and Sam, get too vocal during the meeting. Charlotte believes that user story #2 is clear enough, while Sam thinks it's ambiguous and needs further elaboration. The team moves on to the next user story, ignoring Sam's point of view. Sam accepts the team's decision and remains quiet for the rest of the meeting. At the end of the meeting, the project manager tells Sam that user story #2 could be reviewed during the iteration's first week, when more information is available. Which of the following conflict-resolution techniques did Sam use in this scenario?

A. Smoothing

B. Compromising

C. Forcing

D. Withdrawal

Question 80

You chose for your new project a management framework that is a hybrid of two Agile approaches. The work will be organized in sprints and your team will use a board to display and monitor work progress. Which of the following frameworks are you using?

A. Scrumfall

B. eXtreme Programming

C. Dynamic Systems Development Method

D. Scrumban

Question 81

You and your Agile team are demonstrating a potentially shippable product increment to your project stakeholders. What type of Agile meeting are you conducting?

    A. Review meeting
    B. Standup meeting
    C. Retrospective meeting
    D. Deliverables meeting

Question 82

Four months into a software development project, the project sponsor requests a definitive estimate of when the project will be completed. The most likely estimated duration is 20 days. Which of the following duration estimates will you convey to your sponsor?

    A. 15 - 35 days
    B. 18 - 25 days
    C. 19 - 21 days
    D. 19 - 22 days

Question 83

While performing beta testing with a small number of users, you notice that the web application has defects because of the following reasons:

- User interface and responsiveness issues (20%)
- User experience issues (25%)
- Bugs in functionalities (40%)
- Missing important features (10%)
- Others (5%)

To illustrate these problems, you could use a:

    A. Histogram
    B. Quality Checklists
    C. Scatter Diagram
    D. Flowchart

Question 84

After facing endless issues with one of your project suppliers, you decided to settle the disputes by ending your professional collaboration. Which document should you refer to in order to go through the termination clause as well as the alternative dispute resolution mechanism?

A. Source selection criteria

B. Supplier bid

C. Agreement

D. Project charter

Question 85

As a project manager, along with developing a contingency plan around possible issues, you might also need to create a workaround to deal with _____ once it occurs.

A. Identified & passively accepted risks

B. Unidentified & passively accepted risks

C. Identified & actively accepted risks

D. Unidentified & actively accepted risks

Question 86

Muhammed engaged Outsourci, an offshore software development company, to develop an e-learning platform using the adaptive approach. During the second iteration, Muhammed wasn't satisfied with their work, so he decided to immediately terminate the contract. He only had to pay the incurred costs with no additional fees. What type of Agile contract did Muhammed sign with the supplier?

A. Incremental delivery contract

B. Time and materials contract

C. Target cost contract

D. Early termination contract

Question 87

You are managing a software project following a hybrid approach. During a lessons learned meeting, Rami, one of your team members, complained that every time they submit a new piece of code, they find many errors caused by the code changes made by his fellow developers. So, he suggested testing, updating, and integrating new software code in a more frequent way in order to reduce such errors. Which of the following techniques did Rami suggest?

A. Constant Integration
B. Consecutive Integration
C. Consistent Integration
D. Continuous Integration

Question 88

You're managing a packaging project for which the organization has purchased a custom-built laser printing machine for $130,000 which was later found to be useless. The $130,000 amount represents a _____ cost.

A. Fixed
B. Sunk
C. Indirect
D. Opportunity

Question 89

During an iteration review meeting, the product owner rejected one of the features demonstrated by your development team. What will happen next to the rejected user story?

A. It will be automatically moved to the next sprint backlog
B. It will be deleted from the product backlog and the project
C. It will be updated to address the reasons why it was rejected
D. It will be moved to the product backlog for reprioritization

Question 90

In order to assess your project performance, you calculate both the CPI and SPI. What's your project status knowing that it has a high CPI and a low SPI?

   A. Behind schedule, under budget
   B. Ahead of schedule, under budget
   C. Behind schedule, over budget
   D. Ahead of schedule, over budget

Question 91

Being assigned as the project manager, Juliet noticed that multiple interpersonal conflicts are arising among the team members. What is the best way to handle such conflicts?

   A. You should always smooth conflicts since they distract the team and hinder work progress
   B. You should address conflicts in open meetings so that the entire team can contribute to finding a solution
   C. You should address conflicts proactively and privately, using collaborative and direct approaches
   D. You should be firm and use your coercive power to quickly resolve conflicts

Question 92

You're managing an accounting software development project. In its beta version, some users reported that the software freezes one to three times a day. Since you need more information to fix the problem, you asked the users to fill in a _____ whenever the issue occurs to include information about how the freezing happens and its duration.

   A. Check sheet
   B. Cheat sheet
   C. Checklist
   D. Survey

Question 93

Laura is running a multinational organization. She wants to learn the difference between high and low-context cultures in order to ensure effective communication and avoid doing anything offensive or embarrassing. What is a typical characteristic of communication in high-context cultures?

A. The use of technical means of communication that focus on transferring spoken and written language.

B. Communication is preferred to avoid missing out on a great part of additional information.

C. A conveyed message has little meaning without a full understanding of the surrounding context.

D. To understand a message, there is no need for history or personal opinions.

Question 94

During the risk identification phase, Sonam and her team identified more than 100 risks. She believes that quantitatively evaluating each of these risks will take a lot of time, while not all of the identified risks are important enough to justify such a measure. Instead, what should her next step be?

A. Identifying risk triggers, then quantitatively analyzing only risks with no found triggers

B. Using qualitative risk analysis to prioritize risks for further quantitative risk analysis

C. Qualitatively assessing the probability of each risk, then analyzing only those with high probability

D. Assessing the potential impact of each risk qualitatively, then analyzing only risks with high impact

Question 95

Samuel is a project manager at a company that has been using Agile for over 9 months. When should his company stop tailoring the process?

A. Now

B. Never
C. 18 months
D. 12 months

Question 96
Arnold, a scrum master, is starting a project with a new team and needs to develop an estimate of their velocity. What should he use as a basis for velocity for the first sprint?
A. Forecasted velocity
B. Actual velocity
C. Terminal velocity
D. Cycle velocity

Question 97
You're managing an IT project using the Scrum framework. While the team implements user stories during the sprint, what should the product owner do?
A. Add more features for the team so they can deliver more value
B. Let the team work and respond to any raised questions
C. Protect the team from interruptions and facilitate discussions
D. Monitor the sprint progress and extend it if the team cannot complete the work on time

Question 98
During the elaboration of the quality management plan of your new project, you defined a list of inspection and prevention activities to be conducted at a preset timing. What sets apart inspection from prevention?
A. Inspection focuses on the cause of identified errors, while prevention focuses on resolving them.
B. Prevention focuses on the cause of identified errors, while inspection focuses on resolving them.
C. Inspection keeps errors from reaching the end-user, while prevention prevents them from occurring.

D. Prevention keeps errors from reaching the end-user, while inspection prevents them from occurring.

Question 99

While working on a large project to develop a fingerprint voting system, Lance notices that, lately, a senior developer in his team missed two consecutive deadlines. As the project manager, what should Lance do?

A. Verify whether the developer is a shared resource with another project

B. Give the developer a formal warning via email to improve their work quality

C. Meet with the developer in person and offer support if needed

D. Escalate the issue to the developer's line manager and ask for the concern to be immediately addressed

Question 100

Which of the options below is the project manager's responsibility in Agile?

A. Providing the overall strategic direction

B. Controlling the budget of the project

C. Defining user stories and prioritizing the backlog

D. Ensuring that the team delivers the project according to the defined requirements

Question 101

You are managing a web application project using the Agile approach. During the daily standup, two team members start discussing which JavaScript framework to use: Angular, React, or Vue. What should you do?

A. Let the discussion continue since it's very important

B. Time-box the conversation and suggest that team members carry on with it after the standup meeting

C. Facilitate the conversation and invite the rest of the team to weigh in

D. Share your own opinion on the matter

Question 102

You are in charge of a software development project. Your organization primarily uses agile methods. An intern who has joined your team once asked you: "Typically, what is a User Story?" What should your answer be?

A. A story that refers to the ideal user for your project

B. A day in the end-user life

C. A small, granular unit of work that results in added value to the customer

D. The collection of all the requirements that the customer wants in a project

Question 103

You are managing an internal project to develop Human Resource management software. Since you have adopted the Scrum framework, a sprint planning meeting is held to select user stories. During sprint planning, Reo, one of your team members, insists that a user story concerning a rewards policy implementation should not be brought into the next sprint because it doesn't include enough details on how to set rewards according to employees' different positions and roles within the organization. What is the most likely reason for Reo to push out this user story?

A. The user story doesn't meet the Definition of Ready

B. The user story doesn't meet the Definition of Done

C. The user story involves an unattainable stakeholder demand

D. The user story might result in a waste of time and effort

Question 104

Lara is managing a luxury residency project. Before proceeding with the site excavation process, a government clearance must be issued. What kind of dependency is this?

A. Soft logic
B. Preferential logic
C. External dependency
D. Discretionary dependency

Question 105

Knowledge is sometimes depicted as an iceberg since it involves two categories:

A. Explicit and Tacit
B. Known and Unknown
C. Direct and Indirect
D. Deep and Superficial

Question 106

Control charts are used to routinely monitor quality. You are measuring the response time of your application API, where the lower control limit is 200ms and the upper control limit is 800ms. The first 11 data values are: 790, 700, 750, 750, 716, 770, 620, 200, 444, 104, 404.
What are the problems that need to be solved? (Select two)

A. One of the values is the same as the lower control limit
B. One of the values is out of the control limit
C. Seven consecutive values are between the mean and the upper control limit
D. Two consecutive values are the same

Question 107

All stakeholders are in a meeting to discuss a new project expected to start within one month and to last no less than 10 iterations. One of the stakeholders mentioned that someone should take the responsibility for the development and maintenance of the product roadmap. Who should take this responsibility?

A. Project Manager

B. Team

C. Scrum Master

D. Product Owner

Question 108

You are a team facilitator of a project following the Scrum framework. At what meeting is a potentially shippable product increment presented to the concerned stakeholders?

A. Iteration acceptance meeting

B. Iteration planning meeting

C. Iteration review meeting

D. Iteration retrospective meeting

Question 109

Grade and quality are two of the most commonly used terms in project management on a daily basis. People frequently say that this is a low-grade product, or this is a high-grade product. Which of these is correct with respect to a performed service or a developed product?

A. A low quality can be acceptable, but a low grade is not

B. A low grade can be acceptable, but a low quality is not

C. Both low grade and quality are not acceptable

D. Quality and grade are the same

Question 110

Rita couldn't be happier with her job, as it seems to provide her with almost everything she needs financially, socially, and in terms of self-esteem. According to Maslow's hierarchy of needs, what is the lowest level that should be met before satisfying the other needs?

A. Esteem

B. Physiological
C. Social
D. Safety

Question 111

When you first started managing procurement, a senior expert in your organization advised you to pay attention to oligopoly. Which of the following best describes oligopoly?

    A. There are no sellers in the market, so you need to build the product internally
    B. There is only one qualified seller in the market
    C. There are only a few sellers in the market and the action of one seller impacts the others
    D. Your company policy allows you to contractually engage with only one seller

Question 112

_____ is the technique of applying incremental delivery cycles to perform the work on an Agile project. It is very different from traditional planning since it accepts and expects uncertainty.

    A. Rolling wave planning
    B. Adaptive planning
    C. Progressive planning
    D. Incremental planning

Question 113

Which of the following Scrum meetings centers on the 'product'?

    A. Daily standup
    B. Sprint planning
    C. Sprint review
    D. Sprint retrospective

Question 114

During a meeting with the stakeholders, they inquired about the amount of work completed by your agile team in their last sprint. What information do you need to share with the stakeholders?

A. The sprint's velocity
B. The sprint backlog items
C. The average velocity
D. The forecasting velocity

Question 115

Donald is managing a wind turbine project. The first experiments reveal that the turbine's speed is under the expected value. He and his team attempt to find out the root cause of the issue. Which of the following tools is the most effective for root cause analysis?

A. Five Whys
B. Kano
C. MoSCoW
D. Four Whys

Question 116

You are the Scrum Master for an agile team that is demonstrating a recently developed product increment. Among the deliverables is the product's logo. After explaining the meaning behind his choice for the different elements of the logo, Noah, the project's senior graphic designer, solicited feedback. The product owner appreciated the logo, while the majority of the cross-functional team noted that the logo icon would look better if it was bigger by at least 20%. However, you think that a 10% size increase would be enough to make the logo look better. Which of the following options should be ultimately considered?

A. The icon size should be increased by 20% as per the recommendation of the majority of the cross-functional team
B. The icon size should be increased by 10% as per your recommendation as the Scrum master

C. The icon size should not be increased since the product owner was pleased with the result

D. The icon size should not be increased since Noah is a senior graphic designer, which makes him the most knowledgeable team member in design basics

Question 117

During her long experience as a project manager, Emelie has always settled on the _____ technique for the most long-lasting conflict resolution.

A. Smoothing

B. Confrontation

C. Norming

D. Compromising

Question 118

To calculate the value of your personal computer after two years of use, you apply a straight-line depreciation. Knowing that the current cost of the computer is $1,000 and that its life span is five years, what will be its value in two years?

A. $0

B. $400

C. $500

D. $600

Question 119

At the beginning of the project planning phase, Louis would always emphasize how important it is for all data to be precise and accurate. During one meeting, one of his team members asked if there is really a difference between precision and accuracy. What was Louis' answer?

A. Precision and accuracy are mutually exclusive

B. Accuracy measures exactness; precision measures correctness

C. Accuracy measures correctness; precision measures exactness

D. Precision and accuracy are the same

Question 120

At the end of the project, and during the lessons learned session, you showed the following curve, stating that project expenditures over time represent a(n) _____.

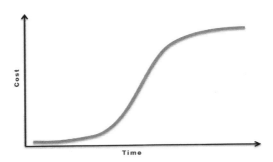

A. Slanted line
B. S curve
C. Z curve
D. Integral curve

Question 121

During your project's planning phase, you found that stakeholders insisted that their conflicting requirements be considered and consolidated. That made it hard to come up with a plan which satisfies all requirements. What is probably the most helpful step to ensure common understanding?

 A. Build focus groups involving concerned stakeholders to discuss and resolve conflicting interests.

 B. Create a document explaining your point of view in detail and ask conflicting stakeholders to review it.

C. Give each stakeholder the opportunity to write a statement of work, and then merge all documents to create the project scope statement.
D. Use your authorization and position as the project manager to choose which objectives to prioritize.

Question 122

Upon conducting a risk identification process, you discovered a technical risk. Thus, you set up a contingency reserve for it. Which risk response strategy consists in creating a contingency reserve?
A. Active risk mitigation
B. Passive risk acceptance
C. Passive risk avoidance
D. Active risk acceptance

Question 123

Zachary is wrapping up a project under contract to build 10 almond cracking machines. According to a contract clause, his customer should be granted a period of two years warranty. What should Zachary's first step be?
A. Collect lessons learned and close the project
B. There is nothing to be done; the legal team should define the warranty clauses
C. Ensure that the warranty clauses are aligned with the final product specifications
D. Verify that there is a sufficient budget to conduct the two years warranty

Question 124

Emery has two potential projects to choose from. The first project has a potential return of $25,000, while the second project has a potential return of $20,000. Emery will eventually select the first project. In this case, the $20,000 will be known as:
A. Sunk cost

B. Opportunity cost
C. Lost cost
D. Potential cost

Question 125

Pax is analyzing accident patterns on a high-traffic flow highway. He draws a scatter diagram to see if there is any connection between drivers' age and the number of accidents. Once the diagram is complete, he notices that all points are scattered in a circular form, as shown in the following diagram. What does it indicate?

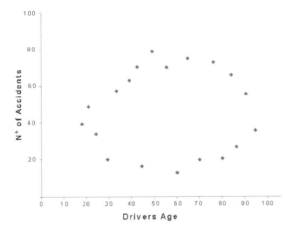

A. No correlation
B. Circular correlation
C. Negative correlation
D. Positive correlation

Question 126

Julian has been assigned to manage a project in Japan. When meeting with the local project stakeholders, he was offered a welcome gift since it's a local tradition to present gifts to guests when meeting them for the first time. What should Julian do about it?

A. He should not accept the gift at any cost
B. He should accept the gift and inform his management
C. He should accept the gift and keep the incident to himself
D. He should accept the gift and politely return it later

Question 127

In a network diagram, the _____ makes the assumption that resources will always be available whenever they are needed.

A. Critical Path
B. PERT Estimate
C. Critical Chain
D. Sprint Planning

Question 128

As a novice project manager, Westly found that working on his interpersonal skills helped him manage stakeholders more efficiently. Which of the following are examples of interpersonal skills? (Select three)

A. Communication style assessment
B. Political awareness
C. Project management certification
D. Cultural awareness

Question 129

In order to respond to the rapidly changing business environment, your organization has decided to use adaptive methods. While attempting to adopt an agile mindset, your project team may use all of the following questions to develop an implementation strategy, except:

A. What work can be avoided to only focus on high-priority tasks?

B. How can the Agile team work in a predictable manner?

C. What work to prioritize in order to obtain early feedback?

D. How can servant leadership help the achievement of goals?

Question 130

Sony, one of your team members, has substantial experience, making her a valuable asset to the project. You recently learned that she'll be promoted to manage a new project within the organization. In this case, you will lose her as part of your team. What should you do next?

A. Give bad feedback about her performance to delay her promotion until your project is completed

B. Inform her about the likelihood of her promotion and ask her to transfer her responsibilities to another team member

C. Ask her to prepare a transition plan, after she gets promoted and receives her transfer orders

D. Hire another resource to replace Sony

Question 131

Daren is managing a hotel interior design project. One month into the project, the sponsor contacts Daren to express their dissatisfaction with the deliverables, which match neither their requirements nor their expectations. How should Daren react?

A. Continue with the next deliverable as he needs to finish the project on time

B. Talk to his manager to discuss the customer concern

C. Ensure that the next deliverables have enough features to meet the client's expectations

D. Perform a scope control to verify if the deliverables meet the project objectives

Question 132

You are using the critical path method to set your project schedule. One of the activities lasts 5 days, with an Early Start (ES) on day 10, and a Late Start (LS) on day 15. What is the activity's total float?

A. 5

B. 15

C. It cannot be determined since Late Finish (LF) is unknown

D. It cannot be determined since Early Finish (EF) in unknown

Question 133

After launching a request for proposals, Diana is assessing four suppliers for her organic catering project. She is going to rank them based on three main aspects: products' quality, production capacity, and cost. Which of the following selection techniques is being used by Diana?

A. Screening system

B. Evaluation criteria

C. Weighting system

D. Contract negotiation

Question 134

Conditions under which you must work and which you cannot control are called Enterprise Environmental Factors. Which of the following is not considered as an Enterprise Environmental Factor?

A. Organization culture

B. Market standards

C. Corporate knowledge base

D. Work authorization systems

Question 135

You are managing a project using the scrum framework. After sizing the selected product backlog items for the next release, you estimated that 5 sprints are needed. However, after running two sprints you find out that your team velocity is reduced for various reasons and that the release deadline can't be met. What should you do next?

    A. Re-prioritize the backlog

    B. Add more developers to the team

    C. Decompose user stories to increase the velocity of the team

    D. Discuss the issue with the product owner to find the appropriate solution

Question 136

For a project in the robotics field, Ava floated a tender for the high-tech equipment needed for her project. To clarify some points, Ava set up a bidder conference. Which steps will be taken by Ava during the bidder conference? (Select two)

    A. Award the contract

    B. Clarify the doubt

    C. Explain the bid terms and conditions

    D. Shortlist the prospective sellers

Question 137

Emily works in an organization that adopts the predictive approach. The project under her management is running over budget, so, it wouldn't be possible to complete it without obtaining more funds. After updating the management on her project status, they ask Emily to present a new budget assessment. Emily estimates that she may need an additional amount of $35,000. This is an example of:

    A. Forecast analysis

    B. Status report

    C. Change request

    D. Progress report

Question 138

Aiden works for a construction company. He is assigned to manage a new highway construction project. In order to help him along with the project, the PMO provides Aiden with their support while requiring him to fully comply with them. What kind of PMO is this?

A. Supportive

B. Controlling

C. Directive

D. Helping

Question 139

When the cost of quality of the project managed by Patricia reached a certain level, her line manager invited her for a meeting to explain the situation. During the discussion, Patricia was asked about the cost of non-conformance. Which of the following are examples of the cost of non-conformance? (Select three)

A. Rework

B. Scrap

C. Warranty work

D. Destructive testing loss

Question 140

You work for a smartphone brand. The company makes a deal with a Chinese manufacturer to produce the phone exterior shell. Upon receiving the Chinese representatives to sign the contract, you hire a translator for those who are attending the meeting but do not speak Mandarin (The official language in China). What is the translator's role in the meeting?

A. Encoding

B. Acting as a medium

C. Removing noise

D. Decoding

Question 141

Upon purchasing software for the project, you identify a probable risk that the software version might be old. In case that risk occurs, you'll just need to go to the settings and update the software version. In this situation, you decide to passively accept the risk. In this case, why is passive risk acceptance the appropriate approach?

- **A.** Because the probability of risk occurrence is very low
- **B.** Because the risk occurrence is difficult to identify
- **C.** Because it would be better to deal with trivial risks when they occur
- **D.** Because the risk is not on the critical path

Question 142

Daisy is managing her first project. She implemented the project management plan meticulously but she is struggling with leading the project team effectively. Talking to her mentor, Daisy was advised to further focus on developing her leadership skills. In this situation, leadership means:

- **A.** Growing an ongoing business over a long period of time
- **B.** Ensuring predictability in an uncertain environment
- **C.** Adhering to standards and procedures
- **D.** Developing a strategy and a vision as well as motivating people

Question 143

During the risk identification process, Ibrahim and his team identified an event which they are not able to evaluate properly to identify its threats or opportunities. Such event is called:

- **A.** Volatility
- **B.** Uncertainty
- **C.** Complexity
- **D.** Ambiguity

Question 144

During a meeting with 15 team members, Jenna the product owner was discussing and collecting ideas about the product requirements. Now they are in the final stage where they are selecting the final idea. As there were many suggested ideas, they decided to vote. After voting, Jenna finds that a particular idea received 9 votes, so she goes with that option. What kind of decision-making is this?

A. Unanimity
B. Majority
C. Plurality
D. Dictatorship

Question 145

Elijah is a product owner for an organization that witnessed major changes on the management level. The new management is not satisfied with the current quality of the organization's products. Consequently, they decided to employ a philosophy to continuously improve all processes and products. What is this philosophy called?

A. Manage quality
B. Just in Time
C. Kanban
D. KAIZEN

Question 146

Maalik is the project manager for a construction project. From past experience, he knows that one main risk that he may face is that the sand supplier may not deliver on time. In the risk management plan, he has already accounted for this risk. The action he will take if this were to occur is to purchase the sand from another supplier. But, in this case, there may be some differences in the sand quality, which would then be a _____ risk.

A. Residual
B. Secondary
C. Compliance
D. Primary

Question 147

Wade is assigned to lead a project abroad. At the start of the project execution, Wade is worried about the country's high levels of violence in public. He gets approached by a local police officer who asks for a private money transfer to ensure the safety of Wade and his team during their stay. How should Wade respond?

- **A.** He should not pay the police officer since it's considered bribery or palm greasing
- **B.** He should not pay the police officer and rather follow the chain of command
- **C.** He should pay the police officer and consider it as a facilitation payment
- **D.** He should pay through an agent considering how suspicious the situation is

Question 148

As a project manager, Abel must assign a complex task to one of his team members. He had to choose between two team members who were both equally capable of fulfilling the task. But, one of them is a member of Abel's in-group while the other one is far more distant. How should Abel behave?

- **A.** Disclose the situation to appropriate stakeholders and solicit a joint decision
- **B.** Choose the in-group person as the trust relationship will benefit the project
- **C.** Choose the person not in his in-group to avoid misunderstandings
- **D.** Assign a third team member to take the decision in order to avoid the conflict of interest

Question 149

Making the transition from a predictive to an agile scrum environment was a big move for Karlie and her team. Switching to a scrum framework, Karlie now conducts different types of meetings to ensure open communication, collaboration, and efficiency. Which of the following meetings is process-oriented?

- **A.** Sprint planning

B. Sprint review
C. Sprint demonstration
D. Sprint retrospective

Question 150

During the project execution, Theodore receives a complaint from one of his team members that the printer along with other electronic equipment are no longer functioning due to excessively hot weather. Deciding to deal with the problem, which of the following are methodological steps Theodore is going to go through while trying to solve the issue? (Select three)
A. Identify the problem
B. Analyze the problem
C. Prevent the problem
D. Check the solution

Question 151

After getting her project approved by the organization's executives, Dakota started estimating the project budget. She is using a bottom-up cost estimation technique to calculate the cost of each activity. The PMO informed her that the value of the management reserve will be 6% of the cost baseline. Which of the following represents the budgeted cost of the project?
A. Cost Baseline + Management Reserve
B. Cost Baseline + Contingency Reserve
C. Contingency Reserve + Management Reserve
D. Cost Baseline

Question 152

Dalila has joined a home appliances production company where quality is imperative for the product. For this reason, the company follows the Six Sigma methodology for its operations. In this methodology, only a _____ percentage of defective products is allowed.

A. 0.0030127
B. 0.0000034
C. 99.69873
D. 99.99966

Question 153
When should you choose a time and material contract instead of a fixed price contract? (Select two)
  A. When you want to limit cost risks
  B. When there is no firm scope
  C. When the work is for an indefinite period
  D. When the scope is precisely defined

Question 154
While reviewing the project team's recent performance report, Ida noticed a major drop in output. To raise the team productivity, she decided to:
  A. Increase the pressure on each team member to meet deadlines
  B. Increase the frequency of status reports and team review meetings
  C. Offer a special reward for the best performing team member
  D. Improve and promote trust and cohesiveness among team members

Question 155
A manufacturing company, working under the predictive life cycle, is implementing a project to create an innovative product using new technology. Details of the component work packages have been defined and constraints for each component have been identified. Top management would like to obtain a precise cost estimate of the project. What estimating technique should the project manager use?
  A. Top-Down
  B. Parametric

C. Bottom-up
D. Analogous

Question 156

When work boundaries are unclear or when the risk is high, you should use a _____ contact. In this contract type, the risk is on the buyer as they pay for all incurred costs.
A. Fixed-price
B. Cost-reimbursable
C. Time and material
D. Flexible

Question 157

Suzan is managing the construction of a new bridge in her city. In order to check how the project is advancing, she sets milestones in the project schedule. What is the typical duration of a milestone?
A. Half the duration of the project
B. The same duration of the project life cycle
C. Zero
D. One month

Question 158

Tom is planning to attend a textile conference not only to get the latest industry trends and updates but also to meet others in the same field. This is an example of:
A. Spying on the competition
B. Research & Development
C. Procurement management
D. Networking

Question 159

During your project closure meeting, your organization's Vice President congratulated you as the PM on completing the project successfully, praising your team's top performers while pointing a finger at the least performing members for failure. What type of leadership is the Vice President showcasing in this situation?

A. Transactional Leadership
B. Laissez faire leadership
C. Interactional leadership
D. Pressure-based power

Question 160
From a project perspective, the guidelines and policies are classified as:

A. Regulations
B. Best practices
C. Assumptions
D. Constraints

Question 161
Sabrina is managing an urban housing construction project. She identified a risk that might affect work execution due to an equipment malfunction. Which of the following risk response strategies will she use to respond to this risk? (Select two)

A. Exploit
B. Enhance
C. Mitigate
D. Eliminate

Question 162
Kehlani noticed that her colleagues tend to waste a lot of office supplies and that inventory is either wasted or underutilized and expired. Therefore, she suggests that inventory management should follow the _____ technique to focus on keeping less inventory and reducing wastage which will eventually improve production and performance.

A. Lean management
B. KAIZEN

C. Kanban

D. Just in Time

Question 163

Amal facilitates a meeting with project stakeholders to discuss a recurring issue with one of the vendors. As a facilitator, Amal should: (Select two)

A. Be in full control of the discussion and its outcomes

B. Be responsible for taking meeting notes

C. Help stakeholders reach common understandings and solve the issue

D. Give guidance as required without interfering

Question 164

Gerard is the project manager of a school construction project. Recently, there was a conflict between two of his key team members. Gerard met with both of them and resolved the conflict through compromise, which led to a:

A. Win-win situation

B. Win-lose situation

C. Lose-lose situation

D. Lose-leave situation

Question 165

You are managing a project using a hybrid method. Upon meeting with the project sponsor, you review how much work the team has and whether they'll be able to finish the project on time. Which of the following point-in-time measurements that you can use for your meeting purpose? (Select three)

A. Product backlog

B. Feature burnup chart

C. Feature burndown chart

D. Lead time

Question 166

As a project manager, no matter which life cycle you adopt for your project, what should always be your top priority?

A. Up to date documentation

B. Efficient collaboration and strong relationships with all project stakeholders

C. Satisfying customers by fulfilling project requirements

D. Elaborating a robust plan and responding to change requests

Question 167

You are managing a project using the Agile approach. When the sprint is almost over, one of your team members informs you that they don't have enough time to properly prepare the demonstration for the sprint review as they are trying to complete the sprint backlog items. What could you suggest in order to avoid such an issue in future sprints?

A. Creating a task for conducting the demonstration

B. Handling the demonstration yourself

C. Delivering a spontaneous demonstration with no preparation needed

D. Delaying the demonstration for a few days to allow your team to get properly prepared

Question 168

Which of the following refers to the start-to-finish time required to develop a potentially shippable product increment?

A. Actual Time

B. Cycle Time

C. Ideal Time

D. Real Time

Question 169

Nada is the product owner for a pregnancy tracking mobile App project. In the planning workshop, Nada ranked the features according to their business value and then presented the prioritized features to the development team. What should the development team do next?

- **A.** Start estimating work
- **B.** Set up another meeting with the customer to capture more details about the features
- **C.** Decompose the features into user stories and tasks
- **D.** Start development work

Question 170

Dominique, who is a scrum master, uses planning poker to estimate user stories. After going through the first user story details, Dominique asked her team members to choose a card as an estimation of the ideal number of days to complete the user story and then to reveal their cards. Since the estimates were vastly disparate, Dominique instantly asked for re-estimates in order to converge team members' estimations. What did Dominique do wrong?

- **A.** The team used ideal days as the unit for the estimates
- **B.** The team re-estimated immediately after everyone revealed their cards
- **C.** Cards shouldn't be revealed
- **D.** Dominique didn't do anything wrong

Question 171

You are managing a big project. You decided to outsource an important part of it to a service provider. To ensure that the selected provider is well suited to your project requirements and quality level, you asked the service provider to go through a _____ first.

- **A.** Logistics phase
- **B.** Transition time
- **C.** Managed supply chain
- **D.** Trial engagement

Question 172

Sophia works within a PMO that is in the process of transitioning to an Agile way of working. The team has shown high resistance to the changes since they are unaccustomed to adaptive approaches. What can the PMO leaders do to encourage adoption?

A. Forge forward and provide point-in-time training on the new methods

B. Train project managers on the adaptive approaches to help on convincing the team

C. Stick to the predictive approach to avoid any conflicts

D. Use a hybrid method that combines both the adaptive and the predictive approaches

Question 173

Emre is a business analyst who gets along with everyone. Thanks to his knowledge of the product, discipline, and ease in getting others to follow his lead, his manager decides to move him into a project manager role. Despite all of his strengths, Emre didn't succeed in his first project. The first major milestone was missed, and the project was way over the estimated budget. What part of the PMI Talent Triangle is Emre missing?

A. Technical project management

B. Leadership

C. Strategic and business management

D. Risk management

Question 174

Indila identified a risk that has a very low probability to occur, but if it occurs it can have a severe impact on the project. In the past Indila accepted these kinds of risks, but this time she followed her organization's culture and planned to hedge the risk. Indila's organization risk attitude is best known as?

A. Risk seeker

B. Risk averse
C. Risk neutral
D. Risk mitigator

Question 175
Managing a high-tech project that involves higher levels of complexity and uncertainties, Everett thinks it is only appropriate to go for an Adaptive life cycle. Adaptive life cycles are also known as: (Select two)
  A. Hybrid life cycle
  B. Project life cycle
  C. Change-driven life cycle
  D. Agile life cycle

Question 176
Working with the predictive approach, which of the following is most true?
  A. Lag may be determined by making a forward pass
  B. Lag is the maximum amount of time a task can be delayed without delaying the early start of its successor
  C. Lag is waiting time
  D. Lag is the maximum amount of time a task can be delayed without delaying the project

Question 177
You're calculating performance measurements based on the following information:
EV = $2,000 and AC = $1,000. What is the status of the project?
  A. The project is ahead of schedule
  B. The project is behind schedule
  C. The project is under budget
  D. The project is over budget

Question 178

Working with the predictive approach, you resort to management reserves to handle which type of risk?
  A. Unknown unknowns
  B. Known unknowns
  C. Business risks
  D. Pure risks

Question 179
One of your team members told you that she thinks you are a great project manager. She explained that she believes you are perfectly adopting various leadership styles depending on the situation you're handling. Which of the following is not a type of leadership style?
  A. Interactional
  B. Transactional
  C. Supportive
  D. Autocratic

Question 180
Sophia, who is one of your team members and a fellow PMP credential holder, is under investigation for violation of the Code of Ethics and Professional Conduct. What should you do?
  A. You should fully cooperate with the investigation
  B. You should tell the PMI investigator it would be a conflict of interest for you to cooperate with the investigation since Sophia is your team member
  C. You should tell the PMI investigator it would be harmful to your project if you cooperate with them
  D. You should cooperate with the PMI investigator by truthfully answering all their questions, but decline to give them any witness statements

Full mock exam - Answers

Question 1 = A
Explanation: The PMI Talent Triangle is made up of three types of skill sets: Technical, Leadership, and Business Management and Strategic skills. A project manager possessing business management and strategic skills should be able to explain the business needs of the project and how they align with the organization's goals.

Question 2 = B
Explanation: The salience model is a method used to classify stakeholders and decide who matters more by assessing their power, legitimacy, and urgency. The model allows the project manager to decide the relative salience of a given stakeholder (PMBOK 6th edition, page 513).

Question 3 = C
Explanation: The best reaction in this situation is to verify the information before taking any action. A violation based only on suspicion should not be reported. Oliver can get the facts right by telling his colleague that he is concerned about his appearance and inquiring if the vendor is the one who provided him with these items. As a project manager, you should never jump to conclusions. You should always double-check facts before reporting a conflict-of-interest situation.

Question 4 = B
Explanation: A Project-oriented organization, or a projectized organization, is one in which a considerable part of its processes and activities take place in the form of projects. There is no defined hierarchy; resources are brought together specifically for the

purpose of a project. When a project is complete, they either get transitioned to another project or released.

Question 5 = B
Explanation: A controlling PMO is focused on two key areas:
- Supporting the organization in applying project management practices.
- Requiring the compliance of those practices.

Such requirements could include the adoption of a particular framework, templates, conformance to governance, forms, etc.
Supportive PMOs only provide a consultative role to projects, while directive PMOs take control of projects by directly managing them.
Agile is a project life cycle and not a type of Project Management Office (PMO).

Question 6 = C
Explanation: An organization's culture, structure, and governance, are Enterprise Environmental Factors that can influence a project's success.

Question 7 = A
Explanation: Douglas McGregor defined two models of worker behavior: Theory X and Theory Y.
Rebecca exemplifies the traits of Theory X managers, who conclude that the majority of people dislike work, lack motivation, and are in constant need of supervision. Theory X managers have an authoritarian style to make their teams work.

Question 8 = A
Explanation: The project manager and Ali are using the Monte Carlo analysis to assess the possible impact of individual project risks and other sources of uncertainty on the project goals. For example, if a particular risk arises, what impact will it have on the project schedule and cost? Monte Carlo provides you with a variety

of potential outcomes and probabilities, allowing you to consider the likelihood of different scenarios. Monte Carlo simulation furnishes the decision-maker with a range of possible outcomes and probabilities that will occur depending on choices of action.

Question 9 = D
Explanation: A team charter is a document that is developed in a group setting to clarify team direction while also establishing boundaries. It is created at the team's forming phase in order to encourage understanding and buy-in. A team charter aligns the team with ground rules, team values, meeting guidelines, working agreements, and other group norms.

Question 10 = A
Explanation: On large projects, one sponsor might not be enough. A Steering Committee is established when a large project involves multiple business units, organizations, or individuals who all have a substantial stake in the project's success and outcomes. The project manager needs to be proactive and respond to this change. The initial communication plan for a single sponsor may not work for this steering committee. In order to ensure effective communication with them, you must understand their communication requirements and preferences.

Question 11 = A
Explanation: Decision trees analysis is used to support the selection of the best course of action among several alternatives. Each of these alternative paths can have associated costs as well as risks including both threats and opportunities. The decision tree reveals the expected monetary value of each branch, allowing the optimal path to be selected.

Question 12 = A

Explanation: Fixed price contracts present the least risk for the buyer. A fixed-price contract is one in which the payment does not depend on the spent time or used resources. It involves setting a fixed price for the service, product, or result defined in the contract.

Question 13 = B
Explanation: A flowchart (also referred to as process maps, progress flows, and progress flow diagrams) graphically displays the logical order of a process (PMBOK 6th edition, page 284). A Pareto chart is displayed as a histogram, representing the most serious causes of an error, while a scatter diagram is used to determine the correlation between two variables. Both diagrams do not show a task or issue's management process flow. Context diagrams, on the other hand, are used to visually demonstrate how a business process, other systems, and people, all interact. Context diagrams can include a business process as one of its components, but they can't provide insight into a particular process flow.

Question 14 = C
Explanation: Since the time zone difference is beyond anyone's control, a compromise should be made to bring some degree of satisfaction to all parties. Each member of the group could give up something, ensuring that no member gets everything. Working towards a compromise is perceived as the best outcome, even if no one is completely happy with the final resolution.

Question 15 = C
Explanation: Surveys and questionnaires are written sets of questions designed to quickly gather data from a large number of respondents who are usually geographically dispersed.

Question 16 = D
Explanation: To persuade an organization to select your project, the business case should be subjected to a cost-benefit analysis in

order to illustrate the benefits of implementing the project by determining its anticipated financial gains and profitability. The Cost-Benefit Analysis is more comprehensive than NPV and ROI, as it attempts to quantify both tangible and intangible costs and benefits.

Question 17 = A
Explanation: The Collaboration/problem-solving conflict resolution technique is based on incorporating multiple viewpoints and insights from differing perspectives. It necessitates a collaborative mindset and open communication to achieve consensus and commitment to an agreement. This approach aims to reach a win-win situation for all involved parties.

Question 18 = C
Explanation: Context diagrams are visual depictions of the product scope, displaying the business system and how it connects and interacts with other systems. It presents the inputs and outputs of the system, as well as its main players, including organizations, other business systems, end-users, etc.

Question 19 = B
Explanation: Student Syndrome is a term used in project management to highlight the ever-increasing habit of putting off work till the last minute, while initially working at a very relaxed pace.

Question 20 = C
Explanation: Backlog refinement provides a chance for the product owner to discuss and address stories' requirements with the team. This can involve discussing requirements, potential approaches, and even estimations in order to end up with a clear vision on how to approach stories.

Question 21 = A
Explanation: Constraints are limitations imposed on a project, such as the scope, schedule, quality, budget, risks, or resources. If assumptions end up being false, it is bad news for the project. However, if constraints turn out to be false, it is a good thing, as it means that your project will be positively affected because constraints are limitations imposed on your project.

Question 22 = B
Explanation: The results are precise because all measurements are close to 4.45 (+ or - 5mm). Precision entails delivering end-products with similar dimensions, which may or may not be close to the required dimensions. Precise measurements are not necessarily close to the target value; they're just close to one another. Accuracy, however, involves creating products with close dimensions to requirements.

Question 23 = B
Explanation: Based on the direction of the hierarchies within the project organization, there are two basic kinds of communication: Horizontal and Vertical Communication. In horizontal communication, you communicate with your peers or people on your level. In vertical communication, on the other hand, the communication hierarchy is from a lower level to a higher level, as shown in the question. "Parallel" and "triangular" communication are made-up terms.

Question 24 = D
Explanation: Taariq is having an informal discussion with the team member. Hallway conversations, cubicle chatting, networking, and all other types of informal communication do not hold any official significance.

Question 25 = A, C, D

Explanation: You shouldn't close the project as key stakeholders are not satisfied. Try to discuss, identify, and resolve any issues or misunderstandings first.

Question 26 = A, B, C
Explanation: Active listening is a skill that can be acquired and developed through practice. Instead of passively receiving the speaker's message, active listening entails paying close attention to what is being said. Active listening involves allowing others to completely express their ideas without interrupting them, asking questions to get a clear understanding of the situation as well as the conveyed ideas, focusing on what is being said by maintaining comfortable eye contact, remaining open-minded about others' opinions, employing paraphrasing skills and feedback, and keeping an eye on non-verbal signs such as the body language and facial expressions of the speaker.

Question 27 = A
Explanation: The most common Benefit Measurement Methods are Cost-Benefit Ratio, Economic Model, Payback Period, Discounted Cash Flow, Net Present Value, Scoring Models, Internal Rate of Return, and Opportunity Cost. The Five whys is not a benefit measurement method; it's rather an iterative interrogative technique used to investigate the cause-and-effect relationships in order to resolve a particular problem.

Question 28 = A
Explanation: Projects are authorized by someone external to the project such as a sponsor, PMO, or portfolio steering committee (PMBOK 6th edition, page 77). Unless the Project Sponsor is part of Senior Management, the project charter should be signed by someone with the authority to assign project resources and name the project manager, i.e., the Project Sponsor. The project manager

or stakeholders may under no circumstances sign the charter to authorize the project.

Question 29 = D
Explanation: The three types of legitimate power are formal power, reward power, and penalty power.

1) Formal or legitimate power is based on the position of the project manager. The assumption that a person has a formal right to make demands gives rise to this form of power. For instance, a CFO holds legitimate authority over an intern who works for them because they are higher in the organizational hierarchy.

2) Reward power stems from giving rewards and it is attached to the formal authority of the project manager. This type of power originates from the ability to compensate another person as it is known that rewards are desirable, and team members tend to support you because they think that you will reward them if they perform well. Non-monetary rewards such as recognition, training recommendations, or a valuable assignment are also common. Criteria for reward should be fair, transparent, and possible for all.

3) Penalty or coercive power comes from the ability to penalize team members. The project manager gains support because project personnel perceives them as capable of directly or indirectly dispensing penalties that they wish to avoid. Penalty power usually derives from the same sources as reward power, with one being a necessary condition for the other.

Other forms of power include Expert power, Referent power, etc.

Question 30 = C
Explanation: The following formula is used to calculate the number of communication channels: Number of potential communication channels = n x (n-1) / 2. In this case: 5 x (5-1) / 2 = 10.

Question 31 = C
Explanation: War rooms, aka situation rooms, or command centers, are spaces where people come together to address issues through enhanced workflows and clear communication. Since they consist of physical rooms, they can't be part of remote teams' advantages. On the other hand, having access to more skilled resources, reducing commute time, and having less travel and relocation expenses are all among the many advantages of employing remote resources.

Question 32 = A
Explanation: Risk transfer involves transmitting future risks from one party to another. A common example of risk transfer is purchasing insurance where the risk of a person or an organization is transferred to the insurance company. Asking the sponsor to deal with the risk is an escalation rather than risk transfer. Other risk response strategies include avoiding, mitigating, or accepting the risk (PMBOK 6th edition, page 443).

Question 33 = C
Explanation: Laissez-faire is a French term that means "allow to act/do". Laissez-faire leadership style is ideal for a highly skilled team since it's characterized by a hands-off approach. Leaders provide all necessary training and support for their employees to enable them to make their own decisions. Project managers opting for this leadership style are comfortable with mistakes, despite the fact that they're the ones held accountable. This leadership approach necessitates a high level of trust.

Question 34 = B
Explanation: Programs are not big projects. While a program mainly focuses on maximizing the organization's profits, project management targets the creation of deliverables that meet and satisfy stakeholder needs.

Question 35 = C

Explanation: You should add the user story to the product backlog and let the product owner decide its priority. When a new requirement is received, it should be added to the product backlog (not the sprint backlog) and then prioritized by the product owner in order to be implemented. It is the responsibility of the product owner to maintain and refine the product backlog. This being said, a request can be made by any stakeholder and a user story can be created by anyone involved in the project and not just the product owner.

Question 36 = B, D

Explanation: Float or slack is the amount of time that a task can be delayed without affecting the deadlines of other subsequent tasks, or the project's final delivery date. The former is known as "free float", while the latter is called "total float". The terms "slack" and "float" are often used interchangeably when a project is scheduled using the Critical Path Method. However, the difference between slack and float is that slack is typically associated with inactivity, whereas float is associated with activity. Slack time permits an activity to start later than anticipated, while float time allows an activity to take longer than it was initially planned.

Question 37 = A

Explanation: The typical size of an agile team ranges from three to nine members. Agile teams should be multidisciplinary (not necessarily have a technical background) and self-organizing (not dependent on the scrum master). Successful agile teams are made up of generalizing specialists/T-shaped people who have deep knowledge in one discipline and a broad ability in the rest of the disciplines. I-shaped, on the other hand, refers to a person with a profound knowledge of one discipline but has no interest or skill in other disciplines (Agile Practice Guide, page 42).

Question 38 = C
Explanation: A benefit-cost ratio (BCR) is used in a cost-benefit analysis to determine the relationship between the eventual costs and benefits of a project. The project is expected to have a positive net present value if its BCR is greater than 1. When selecting a project based on the Benefit to Cost Ratio, always select the project with the highest BCR. Project C has a BCR of 8:2 = 8/2 = 4 which is the highest among all the alternatives.

Question 39 = A
Explanation: Velocity is a measure of the amount of fully completed work in a sprint. Partially done tasks should not be counted. In this case, velocity = 3 + 5 + 8 + 2 = 18 points.

Question 40 = B
Explanation: A Pareto Chart is a vertical bar chart where defects are ranked in descending order according to their frequency of occurrence. The Pareto Chart helps the project team focus on the causes that create the highest number of defects. Pareto's Principle, aka Pareto's Law, states that a limited number of causes will usually produce the majority of defects or problems, which is typically referred to as the "80/20 principle" or "80/20 rule". PERT is not a chart; it's an estimation technique that uses a "weighted" average estimate rather than a simple average ((Optimistic + 4 * Mean + Pessimistic) / 6).

Question 41 = B
Explanation: The 5% limit is the stakeholders' tolerance, which is an enterprise environmental factor. These factors determine how a project manager leads a project. So, it is important for a project manager to have a good understanding of the enterprise environmental factors that could affect their project.

Question 42 = A
Explanation: In the Scrum framework, the sprint planning meeting should include the scrum master, product owner, and the whole scrum team. When needed, other stakeholders can be invited by the team to attend this meeting. During the sprint planning meeting, the product owner identifies the features with the highest priority. The team asks questions to get the necessary understanding to be able to turn high-level user stories into more detailed tasks.

Question 43 = A
Explanation: Regardless of what may happen, you should not offer a bribe. Instead, you should find a legal process to resolve the problem. According to the PMI Code of ethics, the project manager should steer away from any illegal activity such as corruption, theft, embezzlement, fraud, or bribery.

Question 44 = C
Explanation: As a project manager, you cannot leave any stakeholders out of your project. You must find a way to manage them all. Ignoring any of the project stakeholders can be very costly and can dramatically impact the project. You should identify and manage all project stakeholders, regardless of their number. Reference: The PMBOK Guide, 6th Edition, Page: 507

Question 45 = B
Explanation: The iteration review allows obtaining feedback from the product owner and concerned stakeholders at the end of every iteration.

Question 46 = C
Explanation: When you need to hire technical experts, you should use a Time and Materials contract. T&M contract is a hybrid of fixed price and cost-reimbursable contracts. T&M contracts are suitable for projects where the scope of work might change, or

where determining the required duration and material to get the job done might be difficult.

Question 47 = B, C, D
Explanation: Data representation techniques include the stakeholder cube, direction of influence, and salience model. The stakeholder cube adds a third dimension to the analysis of the impact/influence grid. The salience model is used to assess the stakeholder's power, urgency, and legitimacy. The direction of influence, on the other hand, is used to categorize and classify stakeholders on the basis of their influence on the project. Brainwriting is a brainstorming technique for stimulating creativity.

Question 48 = C
Explanation: When an unidentified risk occurs, it is addressed through a workaround. A workaround is an unplanned risk response for dealing with unexpected risks as well as passively accepted risks during project execution (i.e. when there is no predetermined risk response plan put in place).

Question 49 = A
Explanation: Planning poker is a card-based technique that is mostly used for estimating project activities. It is a consensus-based estimating technique. It can be used with story points, ideal days, or any other estimation unit. The estimation is done using poker cards. Team members discuss the feature, asking the product owner questions when needed. Then, privately, each team member picks out one card that indicates their estimate. All cards should be then revealed at once. If all team members select the same value, it will be set as the final estimate. Otherwise, a discussion of the different opinions and estimates will take place again before re-estimating again.

Question 50 = A

Explanation: In portfolio management, a group of related or non-related programs and projects are managed in coordination. Portfolio management is intended to reduce the gap between strategy and implementation by aligning projects to attain business objectives.

Question 51 = C, D

Explanation: Non-verbal communication is used to convey implicit messages. It includes gestures, facial expressions, and paralinguistics such as voice tone or volume, body language, personal space, eye contact, touch, and appearance. These non-verbal signals can provide additional information and meaning to verbal communication. Paralingual communication is non-verbal, but it's not the right answer because the product owner didn't communicate any vocal messages. The scenario doesn't describe active listening either, since the product owner is not interacting or paying attention to the demonstration.

Question 52 = A

Explanation: The iterative method dominates the Agile development process. Each iteration generates the next piece of the development puzzle until completing the final product. Multiple iterations will take place during the Agile development lifecycle.
A typical iteration process flow can be described as follows:

- Analysis: where you define the iteration requirements based on the product backlog, sprint backlog, and feedback from customers and stakeholders.
- Development: which includes design and implementation based on defined requirements.
- Testing: in which Quality Assurance testing takes place.
- Delivery: where you integrate the working iteration into production,
- Feedback: where you receive customer and stakeholder feedback to define the following iteration requirements.

Question 53 = B
Explanation: The burnup and burndown charts are created to identify the amount of workload achieved and how much remains to complete. In a burn-down chart, the line goes downwards, while in a burn-up chart, the line goes upwards, which in both cases illustrates the team's progress. When burndown or burnup charts reveal issues related to sprint progress (which can be caused by both technical or non-technical reasons), a self-organizing team should take corrective actions. In the next retrospective meeting, they need to reflect on what happened and how to better handle issues in the future.

Question 54 = D
Explanation: After 20 days, the total cost of rent will be equal to the equipment's price, i.e., $500 = 20 days x $25.

Question 55 = C
Explanation: Technical Project Management Skills are the skills that Laila is working on. The other two aspects of the PMI talent triangle are Strategic and Business Management and Leadership. Functional Project Management is a made-up term.

Question 56 = A, B, C
Explanation: Examples of forecasting methods are time series, scenario building, and simulation along with regression analysis, expert opinion, and causal/econometric methods. Variance analysis is not a forecasting method. It is the quantitative measurement of the difference between the planned and actual behavior.

Question 57 = B
Explanation: Negotiating is the most important skill for project managers to have when working with extremely limited budgets and resource allocations.

Question 58 = D
Explanation: As a project manager, you must demonstrate transparency regarding your decision-making processes. Communication and reasoning about decisions concerning the project should be well documented and accessible to everyone on the team. Transparency in project communication allows team members to see all aspects and decisions of a project that may affect or be of interest to them.

Question 59 = D
Explanation: Lean principles entail delivering as fast as possible while making decisions as late as possible. Decisions should be based on as much information as can reasonably be gathered to keep all your options open until you must make a decision. There are seven guiding principles of lean practices: Eliminate waste, Amplify learning, Decide as late as possible, Deliver as fast as possible, Empower the team, Build integrity in, and See the whole. Reference: Effective Project Management Traditional, Agile, Extreme, Hybrid by Robert K. Wysocki, pages 360-361.

Question 60 = C
Explanation: Omar should bear in mind that spoken communications can lead to misunderstandings that may not be found in written communications. Intercultural communication commonly entails communicating in a foreign language. Fluently speaking a foreign language is not always enough to fully grasp it. In order to develop intercultural communication skills, comprehending both the language and its cultural context is required.

Question 61 = B
Explanation: When conducting a 100% inspection is not possible, you should opt for the sampling of a certain number from a batch

(also known as a lot) of the items and operate an inspection on the sample. Since testing the filters requires throwing them and not using them on the project, the best course of action is to order more than the required items in order to perform the acceptance sampling.

Question 62 = D
Explanation: Work authorization system is a set of formal documented procedures that establishes how project work will be authorized to ensure the work is done at the right time and in the correct sequence.

Question 63 = C
Explanation: The best course of action, in this case, is to use problem-solving or collaboration techniques to resolve this issue. Therefore, in order to avoid any future problems, disintegration, or rework, organizing meetings is the best option to identify and resolve misunderstandings among team members. The withdrawal technique should not be used in critical conflicts related to project work and deliverables, like in this scenario. Planning risks are supposed to take place in the planning phase. But, since the project is in the execution phase now, you need to follow the established plan and resolve any occurring risks, pre-identified or not. A change request can be issued to manage an impactful risk. The best communication method is interactive face-to-face communication, that's why talking to each team member individually isn't as effective as gathering all team members in one meeting so they can interact with each other.

Question 64 = A, C, D
Explanation: Lessons learned sessions are performed for the purpose of learning from mistakes in order to avoid repeating them in the future. They also serve as an opportunity to gather best practices and build trust with your stakeholders and team

members. Lessons learned should not be used to hold others accountable for mistakes made during the project.

Question 65 = B
Explanation: A project charter is used to formally authorize both the project and the project manager, as well as document the project's objectives and its high-level scope. It also defines the responsibilities and roles of each party involved in the project.

Question 66 = C
Explanation: Statistical Sampling is a technique used to test a small sample of a product in order to make a prediction about the total production. Other statistical sampling methods include systematic sampling, cluster sampling, stratified sampling, and judgmental sampling.

Question 67 = C
Explanation: Screening system is the process of short-listing vendors based on predefined criteria, such as price, technical capabilities, financial capacity, available resources, etc. When certain criteria are more important than others, the criteria should be weighted. Choosing the vendor that responds first to your announcement means you are just selecting and not short-listing vendors. When you only select the first ten vendors who respond to your announcement, it is considered as a screening system. Such a selection, however, is neither rational nor reliable since it won't allow you to short-list the best, most qualified vendors.

Question 68 = D
Explanation: Estimate at Completion (EAC) is calculated by dividing the Budget at Completion (BAC) by the Cost Performance Index (CPI). In this example, EAC = (BAC/CPI) = $900/0.9 = $1,000. Alternatively, you can figure out the right answer without doing any calculation; Since CPI is less than 1, the project is over budget. So,

you need to choose the estimated cost at completion that is bigger than $900. The only available option is $1,000.

Question 69 = A
Explanation: Bids, tenders, quotes, and proposals intersect with each other. Bids or tenders are used when the project is large and the scope of work is clear. Quotes, however, are mainly used to provide the price of particular products or services.

Question 70 = D
Explanation: Unlike predictive approaches, projects that follow adaptive approaches have fixed resources and schedules and flexible scope. While the scope might change in agile projects, teams commit to fixed work iterations known as sprints, when implementing a scrum framework.

Question 71 = C
Explanation: The larger the Net Present Value (NPV), the more profitable the project will be for the organization. A positive NPV indicates that the investment is worthwhile.

Question 72 = D
Explanation: Agile project managers generally follow the servant leadership style, which consists in leading through service to the team. Servant leadership focuses on capturing and addressing the needs of team members in order to achieve good team performance. Participative leadership, aka democratic leadership, involves soliciting team members' input while decision-making rests on the participative leader. Autocratic leadership is when the leader makes all decisions on their own. Transformational leadership is when the leader motivates his team and enhances their productivity through high visibility and communication.

Question 73 = A

Explanation: The "laissez-faire" style has a hands-off approach to management, leaving employees in charge of decision-making. A laissez-faire leadership offers people autonomy as a motivator instead of rewards. This style works successfully when applied to a skilled and talented team. It is not enough for leaders to get the smartest people on board; they must also be able to pick those who can work effectively with others. Autocratic leadership, aka directive leadership, is when the leader takes all decisions by themselves. Democratic or participative leadership involves soliciting team members' input while the leader retains the ultimate decision-making authority.

Question 74 = D

Explanation: There is no limit to the number of portfolios that an organization can manage concurrently. Portfolios should be established as long as there is a need to cluster projects and programs to achieve strategic objectives.

Question 75 = B

Explanation: Trying to convince upper management requires the use of interpersonal skills, which is often a needed skill set when acquiring resources. Dina may lack planning skills since she didn't identify the resource requirement from the beginning of the project, but this situation does not tackle this aspect, nor does the need to respond to the risk associated with adding more resources. In case her manager accepts her request, Dina may not need to go through the hiring process if resources are already available within the organization.

Question 76 = A

Explanation: One of the responsibilities of PMP certification holders is to report violations of the PMP code of conduct. In some cases, however, poor judgments can be corrected. In this scenario, Tom should be given an opportunity to make things right by confessing the truth to his manager. If he doesn't, his colleagues must report his behavior to PMI.

Question 77 = B
Explanation: Tacit knowledge, aka implicit knowledge, is the type of knowledge that can't be transferred to another person by means of writing or verbalizing. Examples of tacit knowledge include insights, beliefs, experience, and know-how. The opposite of tacit knowledge is explicit, formal, or codified knowledge.

Question 78 = C
Explanation: When joining a new organization, it is very important that the project manager grasps the organization's culture. Although talking to the executive managers may help in this matter, understanding the culture, i.e., how the organization operates, its policies, and its appetite for risk, among other things should be the project manager's first priority when joining a new organization.

Question 79 = D
Explanation: Viewing this scenario from Sam's perspective, he had to concede his position to maintain harmony during the meeting. This conflict resolution technique is referred to as withdrawal or avoidance, which results in a lose-leave situation. However, the project manager used the smoothing or accommodating technique, which leads to a yield-lose situation by de-emphasizing differences.

Question 80 = D
Explanation: Scrumban is a hybrid framework that combines Kanban with Scrum. Work is organized in sprints, denoting the use of Scrum. Using a board to display and monitor work progress, on the other hand, indicates the use of Kanban.

Question 81 = A

Explanation: At the end of each iteration, you and your project team should demonstrate a potentially shippable product increment to the concerned stakeholders along with the Product Owner to get their feedback. This occurs during an Iteration Review Meeting. The product owner and stakeholders use this meeting to evaluate the product and release backlog priorities.

Question 82 = D
Explanation: 19 - 22 days fits the criterion as the accuracy of the definitive estimate ranges from -5% to +10%. The definitive estimate is considered the most accurate estimate and is usually developed later in a project. Rough order of magnitude, however, is more common in the very early stages of a project with - 25% to +75% accuracy (15 - 35 days). Finally, the budgetary estimate has -10% to +25% accuracy (18 - 25 days).

Question 83 = A
Explanation: A histogram is a vertical bar chart showing how often a particular variable state occurs. A histogram basically represents data by breaking it down into different categories and helping you make informed decisions. Each column represents an attribute or characteristic of a problem/situation.

Question 84 = C
Explanation: The inclusion of an alternative dispute resolution clause in a procurement agreement as well as a termination clause is a common practice. The dispute resolution process is a resort for the contracting parties to settle disputes and save the time and cost of going to court.

Question 85 = B
Explanation: A workaround is created to deal with unidentified & passively accepted risks once they occur. Workarounds are responses to problems that arise over the course of a project but

were never identified. A workaround is not a planned response because the issues being addressed were not anticipated ahead of time.

Question 86 = B
Explanation: An Agile Time and Materials contract permits the buyer to terminate the contract at any time during the project if they are dissatisfied with the outcome. It is the simplest among agile contracts: The supplier is paid for the time spent delivering a service or creating a product as well as for the used materials in the process. On the other hand, Incremental Delivery Contracts allow the buyer to review contract terms at designated points of their duration; iterations, releases, monthly, quarterly, etc. This means that this type of contract can't be terminated mid-sprint for instance. Early Termination Contract, aka Money for Nothing, allows the buyer to terminate the contract at the end of any Sprint. But, they need to pay the supplier a percentage of the remaining contract value in order to be able to effect early termination. Finally, the Target Cost Contract is based on two values: the "target" cost and the "cap". The target cost is lower than the cap, which represents the maximum sum a buyer can pay. If the project cost is lower than the target cost, the saved amount is shared between both parties. And, if the project cost is higher than the target cost, the extra costs are also shared between them, but only up to the cap. However, if the project cost is higher than the cap, the buyer will support all charges by themselves and the contract will serve similarly as a fixed price contract.

Question 87 = D
Explanation: Continuous Integration dictates that all changes to the application source code base be frequently tested and integrated to reduce risks, improve quality, and establish a quick, reliable, and sustainable development pace. All of the other options include made-up terms.

Question 88 = B
Explanation: Sunk Cost is the investment of resources, money, or time made and cannot be recovered. In this situation, the amount of $130,000 is not recoverable, i.e., sunk cost.

Question 89 = C
Explanation: The right next step consists in understanding why the feature was not accepted in the first place, then moving on to making the required updates. The feature can be moved thereafter to the backlog for reprioritization. Deleting the user story is not a rational choice since the feature has already been developed, which implies that it has an added value to the product.

Question 90 = A
Explanation: Your project is behind schedule and under budget. You can find the Schedule Performance Index by dividing Earned Value by Planned Value (SPI= EV / PV).
If SPI > 1, then the project is ahead of schedule.
If SPI < 1, then the project is behind schedule.
You can find the Cost Performance Index by dividing the Earned Value by the Actual Cost (CPI = EV / AC).
If the CPI > 1, then the project is under budget.
If it is < 1, then the project is over budget.

Question 91 = C
Explanation: Conflicts should be addressed as early as possible using collaborative and direct approaches. It's also recommended that interpersonal conflicts be handled privately among team members rather than in open meetings. Technical conflicts, however, should be discussed in open meetings so that the entire team can participate in finding a solution. When disruptive conflicts persist, you can consider formal procedures, including but not limited to disciplinary actions.

Question 92 = A
Explanation: Check sheets, aka tally sheets, are used to assemble facts in order to facilitate the collection of more data concerning a potential quality issue (PMBOK 6th edition, page 302). A checklist, on the other hand, is used to verify whether a set of required steps has been performed or not.

Question 93 = C
Explanation: High-context cultures use communication that mainly focuses on the tone, meaning, and underlying context of the message. In high-context cultures, what is said does not include all the meaning. The context around who is speaking, the background, and other factors are important to fully understand the message.

Question 94 = B
Explanation: Qualitative Risk Analysis is the process of assessing a risk's occurrence probability and impact. This method helps to focus efforts on only high-priority risks by laying the foundation to perform a Quantitative Risk Analysis.

Question 95 = B
Explanation: A true Agile company will understand that tailoring the process is a continuous task. Projects are undertaken to create a unique service, product, or result which indicates that every project is unique. This is where process tailoring steps in. Process tailoring justifies the fact that the project management processes are not "one size fits all". Every project will have its own process needs and based on that, the project team needs to come up with adjustments to the processes which could include adding, removing, or revising them.

Question 96 = A

Explanation: In a new agile project's first iteration, Forecasted velocity is used since there is no historical data available to help estimate the velocity. After completing the first sprint, you have to use actual velocity instead of the forecasted one. After a few sprints, you have to calculate the average velocity to determine the velocity range. Both 'Terminal velocity' and 'Cycle velocity' are not terms associated with managing an agile project.

Question 97 = B
Explanation: The product owner should let the team work and answer their questions during the sprint. He should not add more work for the team. Facilitating and protecting the team from interruptions are among the scrum master's responsibilities. Besides, sprint length is set at the beginning of the project and typically does not change. Furthermore, any work items that cannot be completed by the team during the sprint should be returned to the backlog and rescheduled for the upcoming sprints.

Question 98 = C
Explanation: Inspection and prevention are both quality assurance techniques. Inspection tries to prevent errors from reaching the customer or end-user, whereas prevention tries to keep the process error-free (PMBOK 6th edition, page 274).

Question 99 = C
Explanation: The project manager needs to understand the reason for recurrently missed deadlines in order to provide appropriate support. As the project manager, you should meet the team member to inquire about what's going on with them and listen attentively. Start out by simply naming the problem and asking for the team member's perspective. You might learn that deadlines weren't as clear as you thought, or that they're facing a roadblock in their work. Talk about the impact of the missed deadlines. The idea here is to demonstrate that these aren't simply arbitrary deadlines; they

have real-world consequences. You should clearly state your expectations for what needs to change in the future. Finally, discuss the next specific steps they'll take to solve the problem – ideally, something they'll come up with on their own, but if they're struggling, you can be fairly directive about what you'd like them to try.

Question 100 = D
Explanation: In Agile, a project manager (also known as scrum master, project team lead, or team coach) is responsible for removing impediments and ensuring that the cross-functional team performs and delivers the product as initially defined by the product owner (Agile Practice Guide, pages 40-41).

Question 101 = B
Explanation: The daily scrum is not considered a problem-solving activity. However, your team can address any problem after the standup meeting with a small group of interested members (Essential Scrum by Rubin, Kenneth S, page 24). For the daily standup to be effective, the Scrum Master or the project manager must focus attention on the core agenda and time-box any side conversations which can always be carried out later, after the daily standup.

Question 102 = C
Explanation: A user story is a brief description of deliverable value for a specific user (Agile Practice Guide, page 155). A user story is not a narrative story about users; it is a small, granular work unit.

Question 103 = A
Explanation: Reo tried to push out the user story because it wasn't ready for implementation as it does not describe how to define rewards according to each employee's role or position within the organization. The Definition of Ready (DoR) represents a checklist of

all the criteria that must be met before a user story can be considered ready to be included in the sprint for execution (Agile Practice Guide, page 151).

Question 104 = C
Explanation: External dependency is the relationship between project activities and external activities that are not related to your project. Even though it's beyond the project team's control, such a dependency should be reflected in the project schedule. On the other hand, discretionary dependencies, also referred to as soft logic, preferred logic, or preferential logic, are not mandatory (PMBOK 6th edition, pages 191-192).

Question 105 = A
Explanation: Knowledge can be classified either as explicit or as tacit knowledge. Explicit knowledge can be expressed and captured using pictures, words, and numbers. Tacit knowledge, such as experiences and beliefs, is more difficult to express or capture.

Question 106 = B, C
Explanation: Here, the first seven consecutive values are found on either side of the mean. This is an example of the rule of seven, so you should identify its cause. Moreover, the second to last request took 104ms, which is below the 200ms lower control limit, so the API response time is out of control.

Question 107 = D
Explanation: In agile, the product owner should be in charge of managing the product roadmap as they are responsible for the product's success. The Product Owner's primary responsibility is to represent the business, which involves the creation and maintenance of the Product Vision, the Product Roadmap, and the Product Backlog.

Question 108 = C
Explanation: It's expected from the Scrum team to deliver shippable product features by the end of each iteration. During the Iteration Review meeting, the Scrum team demonstrates their work to the product owner and concerned stakeholders, in order to get feedback and approval.

Question 109 = B
Explanation: Grade refers to a category or rank given to entities having the same functional use but different technical characteristics. A product can be high-grade (high-end) or low-grade (low-end). A low-grade product is perfectly acceptable, as long as it fulfills requirements. On the other hand, a low-quality product is always a problem and never acceptable. Every item produced must be of high quality regardless of its grade; no one wants a low-quality product. Example: You buy a basic model (low-grade) cell phone with no advanced features, but it works well. Thus, we're talking about a high-quality product. Although it is low-grade, it keeps you satisfied. Reference: PMBOK 6th edition, page 274.

Question 110 = B
Explanation: Physiological factors are at the lowest level of Maslow's hierarchy triangle. Water, food, sleep, shelter, etc. are all vital, basic physiological human needs.

Question 111 = C
Explanation: When there are only a few sellers in the market, any action taken by one of them has an impact on the others, hence the term oligopoly. However, when there is only one seller who dominates the market, it's called a monopoly.

Question 112 = B
Explanation: Adaptive planning allows using iterative development cycles to produce incremental product deliverables as well as

adapting your project plan to changing requirements. Rolling Wave Planning, however, is a form of progressive elaboration that prioritizes near-term plans and "rolls" into the longer term as more details become available. Incremental Planning and Progressive Planning are not terms used in Agile product development.

Question 113 = C
Explanation: The Sprint Review is a product-centric meeting, in which the agile team demonstrates the functionalities they have completed during the sprint, seeking feedback and acceptance from the Product Owner.

Question 114 = A
Explanation: Velocity is the measurement of how much work is completed in each sprint. It is calculated by adding up the sizes of the completed items of the sprint (Essential Scrum by Rubin, Kenneth S, page 119). The sprint backlog is a list of the product backlog items pulled into a sprint, they may not be completed by the end of the sprint. The average velocity is the average of all the previous sprints. The forecasting velocity is used when the team is new to the Agile approach and has no historical data.

Question 115 = A
Explanation: The 5 Whys technique is a simple and effective problem-solving tool. Its primary goal is to determine the precise source of a given problem by asking a sequence of "Why" questions. One of the main factors for the successful implementation of the technique is to make an informed decision based on an insightful understanding of what is happening. Kano and MoSCow are agile prioritization techniques. The "Four Whys" is a made-up term.

Question 116 = C
Explanation: The product owner is the one responsible for accepting or rejecting the demonstrated product increment during

the iteration review meeting. This means that the icon size should not be increased since the product owner didn't ask for any modification. The cross-functional team, including the senior graphic designer, as well as the scrum master, does not have the authority to decide whether a product increment or feature is complete or requires further development.

Question 117 = B
Explanation: Problem-solving or Confrontation is the ideal solution to resolve a conflict. It's a long-lasting conflict resolution technique, as the parties involved get to discuss the problem with an open mind, aiming to find the best solution. Norming is one of the team development stages and not a conflict-resolution technique.

Question 118 = D
Explanation: With the straight-line depreciation method, the value of your personal computer decreases by $200 each year ($1,000 / 5 years). After two years of using it, the computer's value will decline to $600.

Question 119 = C
Explanation: Accuracy implies how close a measurement is to an accepted value. Precision describes the statistical variability of produced measurement (even though it can be far off the accepted value).

Question 120 = B
Explanation: S-Curves visualize the evolution of a project cost over a period of time. The name is derived from the S-shape that data usually form, with a low cost at the project's start and end, and an elevated cost mid-project.

Question 121 = A

Explanation: Focus groups bring together stakeholders and subject matter experts to interactively discuss and learn about their expectations and attitudes towards a proposed service, product, or result.

Question 122 = D

Explanation: Risk acceptance recognizes the existence of a threat, but no practical action is undertaken. Acceptance can be either passive or active. Establishing a contingency reserve, including money to handle the threat if it occurs, is considered an active acceptance strategy. Passive acceptance, however, involves no proactive action apart from a periodic review of the threat to ensure that it does not change significantly.

Question 123 = C

Explanation: Any conducted changes on the product can impact warranty clauses, so Zachary should ensure that the clauses line up with the final specifications. The project closure phase could comprise warranty or support where the project budget is used to fix any defects discovered after the product's shipment.

Question 124 = B

Explanation: $20,000 is the opportunity cost or the "loss" of not choosing the second project. Opportunity cost is known as the loss of potential return by not selecting the second-best project.

Question 125 = A

Explanation: Scatter Diagram with No Correlation or Zero Degree Correlation is when the data points lie in a circle or their spread is random in a way that it's impossible to draw a line across them. A positive correlation is when the number of accidents increases with age, whereas a negative correlation is when the number of accidents decreases with age. Circular correlation is a made-up term.

Question 126 = B
Explanation: Since it is a local custom, Julian should accept the gift and inform management. The project manager should refrain from accepting or offering inappropriate gifts, payments, or any form of compensation for personal gain unless it is in accordance with the laws or customs of the country where the project is being executed. Rejecting or returning gifts may be considered inappropriate and rude in some countries. The best option in such a situation would be accepting the gift and informing your management.

Question 127 = A
Explanation: The critical path drawbacks include the assumption that all project resources are available all the time, not taking into consideration resource dependencies. The critical Chain, on the other hand, takes resource availability into account. The other two options are not related to network diagrams; PERT is an activity estimation technique. Sprint Planning is a Scrum event.

Question 128 = A, B, D
Explanation: All options, with the exception of project management certification, represent interpersonal skills. According to the PMBOK, interpersonal skills include communication styles assessment to identify the preferred communication format, method, and content for each situation, political awareness to help the project manager plan communications according to the project environment, and cultural awareness to understand the differences between groups, individuals, and organizations, thus adapting the project's communication strategy to these differences (PMBOK Guide, 6th Edition, page 375).

Question 129 = B

Explanation: Agile teams don't focus on how to predict the project work; instead, they try to focus on high-priority tasks, getting early feedback, and adopting the servant leadership approach.

Question 130 = C
Explanation: Role, direction, and project transitions are all common occurrences. So, creating a transition plan can ensure the smooth functioning of the project during times of change. The transition plan outlines the hand-off process and defines all the priorities, goals, and strategies for a successful shift. However, you can only ask Sony to prepare it when her promotion becomes official through a transfer order for instance. Transferring responsibilities or hiring other resources should not be based on a mere possibility. Giving bad feedback about your team member's performance to delay her promotion until your project is completed is neither appropriate nor ethical.

Question 131 = D
Explanation: Project scope verification or control involves reviewing deliverables to make sure that each is appropriately completed as per requirements. Any discovered inconsistency or dissimilarity should be rectified before seeking the sponsor's formal approval through the "validate scope" process.

Question 132 = A
Explanation: Total Float = Late Start date – Early Start date = 15 - 10 = 5

Question 133 = C
Explanation: Since Diana is ranking suppliers using specific criteria (aka evaluation criteria), it means that she is using the weighting system by scoring their performance on each criterion. Diana is not doing any contract negotiation yet. Plus, she is not

using a screening system because she is not eliminating sellers who do not meet particular conditions.

Question 134 = C
Explanation: Corporate knowledge base is part of the Organizational Process Assets. Enterprise Environment Factors (EEFs), however, include all procedures, policies, and legislation that has an impact on how you manage a project. Examples of EEFs include Organizational culture, Market standards and conditions, Codes of conduct, Quality standards, Work authorization systems, Risk databases, etc. (PMBOK 6th edition, pages 38-39).

Question 135 = D
Explanation: You should inform the product owner and discuss with them the different options and measures. If the release date cannot be changed then the product owner could re-prioritize the release backlog. You, as a project manager or scrum master, should not reprioritize the backlog. Additionally, decomposing user stories cannot result in more productivity nor increase your team's velocity since the amount of work will still be the same. Adding more developers to the team may increase the velocity, but it will increase the cost as well. Plus, this option should be approved by the product owner, and could only be adopted when the release date and scope are more important than the cost.

Question 136 = B, C
Explanation: Bidder conference, aka contractor conference or vendor conference, is arranged to ensure that the sellers have a common understanding of the procurement requirements. During the conference, the project manager and the stakeholders will discuss what they want from the vendors and answer any questions they have. In a bidder conference, you do not shortlist the prospective sellers nor award the contract.

Question 137 = A
Explanation: The project budget might change as the project progresses. In this case, Emily informed management about the new forecasted budget; (BAC + $35,000), which is known as EAC (Estimate at Completion).

Question 138 = B
Explanation: A controlling PMO provides support and requires that this support should be used. Requirements might include forms, templates, conformance to governance, etc. The two other PMO types are: supportive and directing (PMBOK 6th edition, page 48).

Question 139 = A, B, C
Explanation: Destructive testing loss is an example of the cost of conformance, the rest are examples of the cost of non-conformance. Cost of Non-Conformance represents the expenses arising due to the non-conformance to the quality requirements.
Cost of Non-Conformance can be divided into two categories:
1. Internal Failure Costs are incurred when defects in the deliverables are detected internally (i.e. not yet presented to the customers) including defect repair and rework.
2. External Failure Costs are incurred when defects are found after the deliverables have been delivered to customers and in actual use (this is the worst kind of quality costs) including warranty work, liabilities, and loss of business goodwill.

Reference: PMBOK 6th edition, page 283.

Question 140 = D
Explanation: The message is in Mandarin, which a lot of meeting attendees don't understand. The translator is translating the message to a language they can understand; he/she is decoding the message. Decoding is when the received data is translated into a form that the receiver can understand.

Question 141 = C
Explanation: Passive risk acceptance is an appropriate approach when it is best to handle the risk as it occurs. No proactive action is needed for passive acceptance other than periodically reviewing the threat to ensure that it does not change significantly (PMBOK 6th edition, page 443).

Question 142 = D
Explanation: Successful leaders are able to communicate the vision for a project to their team so that everyone has a shared vision of the bigger picture. When the whole project team understands the project vision, individuals are better able to see where they fit in and how each of their roles contributes to the project's success.

Question 143 = B
Explanation: Uncertainty refers to a lack of definite knowledge, a lack of sureness. In uncertainty, the outcome of any event cannot be guessed or measured; you lack information on the event. Unlike ambiguity, uncertainty is not an unknown risk. Complexity, however, can be defined as a situation where the interconnectedness of variables is so high, that the same conditions and inputs can lead to very different outputs or reactions. Volatility is when a challenge is unstable or unexpected and may be of unknown duration, but it is not necessarily difficult to understand. Reference: Managing in a VUCA World by Oliver Mack, Anshuman Khare, Andreas Krämer, and Thomas Burgartz, pages 6-7.

Question 144 = B
Explanation: Voting is a technique for collective decision-making which can be used to generate and prioritize project requirements. Unanimity, plurality, and majority are examples of voting techniques. A majority decision necessitates getting the support of more than 50% of the group members.

Question 145 = D
Explanation: KAIZEN means 'improvement' in Japanese. KAIZEN is a practice and a philosophy that focuses on the continual improvement of productivity throughout all aspects of life. KAIZEN aims to create a team atmosphere, improve everyday procedures, ensure employee satisfaction, and make a job more fulfilling.

Question 146 = B
Explanation: A secondary risk is a risk caused by a response to a primary risk. Alternatively, the secondary risk would not exist if the risk response was not taken.

Question 147 = B
Explanation: In such situations, Wade should not pay and should follow the chain of command and solicit their support in providing security to the project team. This situation could be considered as bribery or at least palm greasing. Nevertheless, the project manager should act proactively and take all security measures.

Question 148 = A
Explanation: As the PMI code of ethics indicates under the Fairness chapter, Abel should disclose any potential or real conflict of interest to stakeholders (PMI Code of Ethics and Professional Conduct, page 5).

Question 149 = D
Explanation: The Sprint Retrospective is a process-oriented meeting that is held at the end of each iteration. Its purpose is to explicitly reflect on the most significant events that have occurred during the current iteration in order to make decisions on how to improve processes during the next iteration. Sprint review or demonstration, on the other hand, is a product-oriented meeting.

Question 150 = A, B, D
Explanation: The project manager should use methodical steps to deal with problem-solving, which can include: Identifying the problem of specifying the problem, defining the problem and breaking it into smaller manageable problems, investigating by collecting data, analyzing to detect the root cause of the problem, solving by choosing the suitable solution, and checking the implemented solution to determine whether the problem has been fixed or not. Preventing the problem is not correct because the problem already took place.

Question 151 = A
Explanation: Management reserve is needed as part of the project budget to address unforeseen risks. The difference between the project budget and the cost baseline is management reserve. The cost baseline is the total of all the approved budgets for the scheduled activities. To put together the project budget, the management reserve is added to the cost baseline. The contingency reserve is part of the cost baseline (PMBOK 6th edition, pages 245-252-255).

Question 152 = B
Explanation: Six Sigma is a quality management methodology used to help businesses improve current processes, products, or services by discovering and eliminating defects. The Six Sigma process is expected to have 99.99969% defect-free products (or 0.0000034% of products can have defects).

Question 153 = B, C
Explanation: A time & material contract is an agreement in which the contractor is paid on the basis of the actual labor cost (in hourly rates – man-hour) together with materials and equipment usage. This contract type is used when there is no firm scope, or the work is for an indefinite period (i.e. ongoing development of the product).

Question 154 = D
Explanation: Improving feelings of trust and cohesiveness among team members initially leads to improved productivity. Team cohesion occurs when people feel fulfilled and driven to achieve a common goal. Increasing team cohesion naturally helps you boost employee engagement by creating positive relationships, team goals, and shared values that increase commitment.

Question 155 = C
Explanation: The Bottom-up estimation technique is used when requirements are decomposed into small, feasible work pieces which are then aggregated to estimate the cost of the entire project. The Bottom-up technique provides a precise estimate of both the project cost and duration.

Question 156 = B
Explanation: Under a cost-reimbursement contract, the buyer takes on more risk as the seller charges for all legitimate expenses related to completing the product or service, as well as a fixed fee as profit for their work. The buyer assumes the risk in case the scope costs more than estimated. However, in a Fixed Price Contract, the buyer doesn't take any risk, while in a Time and Material contract the risk is shared between the buyer and the seller (because the buyer's cost might escalate due to the undetermined duration of the contract, and seller's profit might decrease due to potential material/resources cost increase over the project life-cycle). Reference: PMBOK 6th edition, page 472.

Question 157 = C
Explanation: The duration of a milestone is zero because it denotes an achievement or a point of time in a project, such as the completion of a deliverable (PMBOK 6th edition, page 186).

Question 158 = D
Explanation: Attending a conference is considered networking, it is not spying on the competition. To network means to connect with people. The classic way is to meet face-to-face, either in a formal or an informal frame. Networking can also be done through social media platforms as they provide an opportunity to network with those in your field on a constant basis. On a smaller scale, examples of networking include informal conversations, committee gatherings, luncheons, and so on.

Question 159 = A
Explanation: Transactional leadership is when the leader uses reward and punishment to motivate their team. The disadvantage of transactional leadership is that it can't keep followers motivated in the long run.

Question 160 = D
Explanation: Project constraints are the restrictions that limit the project in a certain way. A cost restriction, for instance, means that the project is limited by its allocated budget or resources. Other constraints include policies, standards, guidelines, etc.

Question 161 = C, D
Explanation: This is an example of negative risk; therefore, Sabrina should use either the mitigation strategy to minimize the risk impact or the eliminate strategy to completely avoid the risk. The other two strategies, exploit and enhance, are positive risk response strategies.

Question 162 = D
Explanation: Just in Time (JIT) is the technique of using resources only when they are needed. For instance, instead of acquiring a large inventory of spare parts to be used in manufacturing, you only obtain parts when needed. Lean management is a philosophy that

calls for eliminating waste as one of its principles. Unlike JIT, Lean management is not a technique. Kanban, on the other hand, is a lean method for managing and improving work. KAIZEN is a quality management philosophy that consists in continuously applying gradual improvements to enhance efficiency, business, and performance.

Question 163 = C, D
Explanation: Facilitation means assisting others in dealing with a process, reaching an agreement, or finding a solution without getting personally or directly involved in the process, discussion, etc. For the facilitator to maintain an impartial position, they should approach the discussion as an unbiased voice.

Question 164 = C
Explanation: As a conflict resolution technique, compromise results in a lose-lose situation since both involved parties have to give something up to appease the other party. As a result, neither party really gets all of what they want. Typically it results in resentment affecting productivity when obtaining buy-in from all parties involved. The other resolution types are:
- Forcing: which leads to a win-lose situation.
- Smoothing: which leads to a yield-lose situation
- Withdrawing: which leads to a lose-leave situation
- Problem-solving or confrontation: which leads to a win-win situation.

Reference: Guan, D. (2007). Conflicts in the project environment. Paper presented at PMI Global Congress 2007.

Question 165 = B, C, D
Explanation: Feature burnup/burndown charts, lead time, and cycle time provide in-the-moment measurements, giving insight into the team capacity and the schedule predictability. Lead time is the duration between task creation and task completion. Cycle time,

however, is the duration between when the team starts working on a user story and when it's delivered to the end-user. The product backlog is not a measurement, it's rather a list of the work that needs to be done to develop the final product.

Question 166 = C
Explanation: As with any business, customers or sponsors have to be the highest priority when delivering a product. It's not enough to deliver a product that simply works; the product must work for and do what the customer or the sponsor needs it to do.

Question 167 = A
Explanation: The creation of a task to demonstrate the product and make it part of the sprint allows the team to get the necessary time to prepare for the demonstration. The sprint demo shouldn't take up too much of a Scrum team's time. Time shouldn't be spent putting long slide decks together; the focus should be on the work and the demonstration should only include stories that meet the team's definition of Done. Typically, a day or two before the end of the sprint, a project manager holds a short demo run-through and makes notes on anything they need to set up in order to make the demo flow well.

Question 168 = B
Explanation: The time it takes to complete a task from start to finish is referred to as cycle time. Actual Time and Real Time are used synonymously as they both refer to the daily period during which team members are productively working on their assigned tasks. When you make the assumption that your Agile team is fully productive and that they're not being interrupted by attending meetings or checking emails, you're referring to Ideal Time or Ideal Days.

Question 169 = C

Explanation: The team's next step should involve continuing with the planning activity through decomposing features into stories and tasks. During the sprint planning workshop, the product owner determined top priority features for the Agile team. The team should ask for more details in order to turn a high-level user story of the product backlog into more precise tasks to accomplish during the sprint. The product owner doesn't have to describe every item being tracked on the product backlog. Such decomposition is part of adaptive planning.

Question 170 = B
Explanation: The team misses out on the benefit of discussing the reasoning behind their estimations when they immediately carry on with re-estimation. Often, estimates vary in the first round of planning poker. The team should discuss the story and their estimates. After the discussion, each team member re-estimates the story in question again by selecting a card. The process should be repeated until reaching a consensus. The number of rounds of estimation may vary from one user story to another.

Question 171 = D
Explanation: Some projects engage several candidate sellers for initial paid work before making the full commitment. This allows the buyer to evaluate potential partners, while simultaneously making progress on project work.

Question 172 = D
Explanation: Transitioning a team to Agile could be difficult and confusing when they are not accustomed to or familiar with this approach. One of the most effective transition methods is the adoption of a hybrid approach that combines both predictive and adaptive methods as a means of introducing Agile to the team.

Question 173 = A

Explanation: The PMI Talent Triangle consists of three sets of skills: leadership, technical project management, and strategic and business management. Since the project is over budget and behind schedule, Emre is most likely lacking formal project management knowledge and training.

Question 174 = B
Explanation: Averse means opposing. A risk-averse organization is not very supportive of or creative towards risks. Such organizations usually try to avoid risks unless there is a good reason to accept them.

Question 175 = C, D
Explanation: Adaptive life cycles are also called change-driven or change-focused methods or agile as they're quite adaptable to changes.

Question 176 = C
Explanation: Under a predictive approach, Lag is when an activity is complete and there is a delay before the subsequent activity starts. For example: to paint a room, you will first apply the primer coating, then you have to let it dry for two days before applying the final coat of paint. These two days of waiting for the primer coat to dry are called Lag Time.

Question 177 = C
Explanation: The CPI (Cost Performance Index) is a measure of the conformance of the actual work completed (EV, Earned Value) with the Actual Cost (AC) incurred:
CPI = EV / AC = \$2,000 / \$1,000 = 2 which means that the project is under budget.
The Schedule Performance Index is a measure of the conformance of actual progress to the planned progress (SPI = EV / PV). Since

the PV is unknown, we can't figure out if the project is behind or ahead of schedule.

Question 178 = A
Explanation: The management reserve is used to manage the unidentified risks, aka "unknown-unknown". The management reserve is part of the project budget, but it's not part of the cost baseline. The management reserve is not an estimated reserve; it is rather defined according to the organization's processes and policies. It can represent 5% of the total project cost for instance. As the name indicates, this reserve is controlled by the management, not by the project manager. Therefore, any usage of this reserve for unidentified risks should be approved by the management.

Question 179 = C
Explanation: Supportive is a type of PMO, not a leadership style. A situational leader is a project manager who employs a variety of leadership styles depending on the situation. Leadership styles include Directing, Facilitating, Coaching, Autocratic, Consultative, Consultative-Autocratic, Consensus, Bureaucratic, Democratic or participative, Analytical, Driver, Influencing, Laissez-faire, Transactional, Servant, Transformational, Charismatic, and Interactional.

Question 180 = A
Explanation: The Code of Ethics and Professional Conduct requires that you cooperate in any investigation concerning ethics violations and in collecting information related to the
Violation.

Full-Exam Result Sheet

Assign "1" point to each question answered correctly, and then count your points to get your final score.

1. ____	21. ____	41. ____	61. ____	81. ____	101. ____	121. ____	141. ____	161. ____
2. ____	22. ____	42. ____	62. ____	82. ____	102. ____	122. ____	142. ____	162. ____
3. ____	23. ____	43. ____	63. ____	83. ____	103. ____	123. ____	143. ____	163. ____
4. ____	24. ____	44. ____	64. ____	84. ____	104. ____	124. ____	144. ____	164. ____
5. ____	25. ____	45. ____	65. ____	85. ____	105. ____	125. ____	145. ____	165. ____
6. ____	26. ____	46. ____	66. ____	86. ____	106. ____	126. ____	146. ____	166. ____
7. ____	27. ____	47. ____	67. ____	87. ____	107. ____	127. ____	147. ____	167. ____
8. ____	28. ____	48. ____	68. ____	88. ____	108. ____	128. ____	148. ____	168. ____
9. ____	29. ____	49. ____	69. ____	89. ____	109. ____	129. ____	149. ____	169. ____
10. ____	30. ____	50. ____	70. ____	90. ____	110. ____	130. ____	150. ____	170. ____
11. ____	31. ____	51. ____	71. ____	91. ____	111. ____	131. ____	151. ____	171. ____
12. ____	32. ____	52. ____	72. ____	92. ____	112. ____	132. ____	152. ____	172. ____
13. ____	33. ____	53. ____	73. ____	93. ____	113. ____	133. ____	153. ____	173. ____
14. ____	34. ____	54. ____	74. ____	94. ____	114. ____	134. ____	154. ____	174. ____
15. ____	35. ____	55. ____	75. ____	95. ____	115. ____	135. ____	155. ____	175. ____
16. ____	36. ____	56. ____	76. ____	96. ____	116. ____	136. ____	156. ____	176. ____
17. ____	37. ____	57. ____	77. ____	97. ____	117. ____	137. ____	157. ____	177. ____
18. ____	38. ____	58. ____	78. ____	98. ____	118. ____	138. ____	158. ____	178. ____
19. ____	39. ____	59. ____	79. ____	99. ____	119. ____	139. ____	159. ____	179. ____
20. ____	40. ____	60. ____	80. ____	100. ____	120. ____	140. ____	160. ____	180. ____

Total:

N° of Correct Answers	% of Correct Answers
--------- / 180	---------

Did this book help you prepare for your PMP certification exam? If so, I'd love to hear about it. Honest reviews help other readers find the right book for their needs.

ABOUT THE AUTHOR

Yassine is a PMP® certified Instructor & Author with more than 10 years of experience in the IT field, moving up in his career through multiple positions like a Business Developer, Account manager, Functional consultant, Product owner, Office manager, up to being currently a Project manager.

Managing and leading both on-site and remote projects, in the public and private sectors, Yassine is passionate about helping and sharing his Project Management expertise and knowledge.

Relying on his academic background along with his real-life experience managing projects in Telecommunications, Retail, Financial Services, and more, Yassine aims to present practical rich content suitable for beginners as well as professionals in the PM field.

Yassine strongly believes in the practical methodology, offering easy to apply knowledge that he is certain about its efficiency considering that he practices what he preaches in his daily position as a Project Manager.

Printed in Great Britain
by Amazon

68418922R00145